MW01166669

IN THE NAME OF MY FATHER

An Inspirational Memoir

By
Pollyanna Prosper-Barnes, Ph.D.

TEACH Services, Inc.
Brushton, NY

**PRINTED IN
THE UNITED STATES OF AMERICA**

World rights reserved. This book or any portion thereof may not be copied or reproduced in any form or manner whatever, except as provided by law, without the written permission of the publisher, except by a reviewer who may quote brief passages in a review. The author assumes full responsibility for the accuracy of all facts and quotations as cited in this book.

2010 11 12 13 14 · 5 4 3 2 1

Copyright © 2010 Pollyanna Prosper-Barnes and
TEACH Services, Inc.
ISBN-13: 978-1-57258-620-8
Library of Congress Control Number: 2010924773

Cover Design by Richard White of Rowhouse Advertising & Design
(rowhouseadv.com)
Edited by Gabrielle Barnes of Diction Media Group LLC

Published by

TEACH Services, Inc.
www.TEACHServices.com

I write this book in the name of my earthly father who lived in the name of his heavenly Father.

This book is dedicated to my wonderful mother, Naomie Prosper, for her unconditional love to Papa, my siblings, and me; and to my husband, Baldwin S. Barnes, for his love and devotion and for being a great father to our children. Thank you both.

Contents

INTRODUCTION

Naasson Belizaire-Prosper was the son of Meshack and Marie-Lezynska Belizaire-Prosper. He lived for seventy-four years on the face of the earth. He married Naomie, and they lived together for forty-nine years and two months. They had eleven children, two of which died at an early age. During those seventy-four years of life, he loved his wife, parented his children, and devoted his life completely to God, to the service of humankind, and to the Seventh-day Adventist Church. This book, *In The Name of My Father*, offers a window into the private life of a public man and the impact he had on me.

In October 1998 the doctor revealed to my family that my father had a terminal brain tumor. The prognosis was that Papa would live for three to six months. The news of his imminent death shocked every cell in my body and put me out of balance. I was numb, unable to conceive my life without Papa. He played such a significant role in every part of my existence. How was I going to face the future? How could I accept his fate and go through the excruciating pain I was sure to experience? With the thought of life without Papa being unbearable, I began to reflect on our life together, writing things down in a journal. I began recapping my life with him soon after the diagnosis. Papa was buried on Father's Day, June 20, 1999. (Father's Day has never been the same since.) I stopped journaling one year later on June 20, 2000. This purging process prepared me to face his looming death and helped me heal after his departure.

Even before his illness, I had intended to write a book about my father, the two of us had planned that I would write his biography. The idea of turning the journal into a book began to permeate my thoughts. As I shared my journaling journey with my dearest friend, Joy, and recounted some of the stories that I had registered in it, she promptly encouraged, "You should turn this journal into a book!" Even though I initially wrote for my own sanity and healing, I started the arduous work of reliving the experiences to share with others as an inspiration. It was at times very painful, and whenever the project became emotionally unbearable, I retreated from it to recuperate.

After a while, I realized that I didn't want the book project to end because it would mean permanently closing the door on my life with Papa. As long as I was working on it, my father was alive to me. The memories felt so real that I kept him alive in my mind and heart. I didn't want to let him go. In a conversation with my friend Todd, he encouraged me to finish the project. He said, "Pollyanna, you have to write this book. Don't keep your father to yourself. A man like that should be shared with the world. Share your father with the world."

With this as my mission, I began to write with a twofold purpose. Firstly, I wanted to honor my father by sharing him with the world. I wanted readers to meet a man who lived a life of integrity and taught his children to do the same. I wanted his story to inspire readers to live a powerful Christian life. Secondly, I wanted to motivate fathers to get involved in their children's lives because fathers are so crucial to the balanced development of their daughters and sons. The quality of a girl's relationship with her father will determine the quality of her relationship with her husband and with men in general. Papa's parenting methods may not all be as effective today as they were in his time, but the principles are universal and timeless. Children are the product of their home environment. Parents are the most important and impactful people their children will ever interact with. Today's parents will do well to intentionally imprint well-rounded Christian principles and values on their children's mind and heart.

Both of my parents contributed to who I am today. Maman, my mother, has taught me valuable life lessons and partly shaped my character. She has been a constant believer, supporter, and influence in my life. She believes that I can be or do anything that I set my mind to and has continued to nurture that in me. She impacted me greatly. However, it was Papa who sculpted me into who I am and in the process helped to build up my self-esteem. He caused me to believe in myself in every aspect of my life by affirming me, challenging me, building me up, and stretching me. He made me believe that I was special and I could become anything I wanted to. He taught me how to live life from the perspective of a princess: I am a child of the King. He taught me structures in which I can operate effectively and successfully. He taught me social graces that allowed me to interact with and access people. Best of all, he taught me to be a Christian and a servant of God.

I close this chapter of my life by publishing *In The Name of My Father.* The timing is fitting because it commemorates the tenth anniversary of Papa's death. My love for him will never end, and the memory of him will remain vivid in my mind and heart. So there you have it: this book chronicles the life of my father—the strongest, most definitive influence in shaping me into who I am—through my eyes. I introduce you to my papa.

ONE

NAMED TO BE

Dear Nao:

I am sorry that I could not be with you to welcome our new baby into this world. I am pleased to know that both of you are well. God has blessed us with another daughter. May His name be praised! I don't know what He has in store for her. She is born in a time when we are experiencing severe financial difficulties in our life together, but I know that God will provide.

*We will name her **Polly-Anna**. My hope is that when she will face hard times in life, she will be able to look for the good and play **The Glad Game**.*

On my thirtieth birthday, my mother came into my room and gently placed a folded letter in my hand. She explained that the day I was born Papa was out of town working as a literature evangelist. (As a literature evangelist/colporteur, he sold religious books for a living to help spread the Gospel). Maman sent him a telegram informing him of my birth. He responded immediately, and above is a section of the letter he wrote to her. After reading the letter, I exclaimed to her, "You saved this letter all these years!" I

1

stared at it in amazement. "This letter is part of my history. It is as old as I am!!" What an incredible gift!

The letter in my hand felt as sacred as the Scrolls of Qumran. The pages were tattered, the ink smeared, and some words faded. I felt a strong sense of who I was in holding those sacred sheets. It was inexplicably precious to me. I thanked Maman for saving it all these years and for sharing with me the definition given to me in my name at birth.

Maman took a moment to reminisce on my childhood. She described my attitude as a child. I was a happy and positive child. I naturally played the "glad game." She said that when she gave me food I didn't like, I ate it saying, "If I am happy with the things I don't like, God will bless me with the things I like." She pointed out that I also loved to say, "If I am faithful with little things, God will bless me with big things."

Maman revealed, "I admire the way you view things, the way you handle situations with such a positive attitude. You are happy in times of abundance and scarcity. That was your father's wish for you and that is who you have become. A spirit like yours pleases God. Look how God is blessing you now. "

❧   ❧   ❧

Until that day, I didn't realize that Papa named me after Pollyanna from Eleanor Porter's book. I don't recall ever having a conversation with him about the origin of my name. I could have, but I may have been too small to remember. But all along, I assumed that Papa had created my name by combining the names of two of his friends: Miss Polly, an American nurse in Haiti, and Anna, a friend who later became my fifth grade teacher. Since most of my siblings are named after someone, I figured that the same applied to me. I was familiar with the story of Pollyanna because Papa gave us the book; however, I didn't make the connection because he wrote my name Polly-Anna.

In the novel, Pollyanna is the daughter of a poor missionary,

Reverend Whittier, who preached sermons of gladness to everyone. He encouraged people to embrace the practice of being glad and to refer to the eight hundred plus texts in the Bible where God's people are encouraged to "rejoice and be glad. "

Pollyanna developed a happy and sunny disposition. She was the epitome of optimism. Her father created a game called "The Glad Game" as a result of a disappointment that Pollyanna had experienced one Christmas. She wanted a china doll; instead, she received a pair of crutches. She was devastated. In an effort to help her recover from her disappointment, her father created a game, encouraging her to name one good thing about receiving the crutches as a gift. Consequently, Pollyanna developed the attitude of continuously looking for the bright side in every situation.

The book's popularity resulted in the word Pollyanna being added to the English dictionary; the entry is defined as "a person who always finds good in everything; a girl or woman who is untiringly cheerful and optimistic in the face of difficulty, trouble and disaster" (*The World Book Dictionary*).

Papa named me into existence. He wished me to be optimistic and to play "The Glad Game" whenever I faced challenges in life. He wanted me to look for the good in everything. I believe I fulfilled his wish. I am optimistic. It is interesting how a name can influence a person's personality. Pollyanna Prosper; the Prosperous Pollyanna. Whichever way you look at it, what a name! I love my name and it fits me perfectly.

Names signify character. They signify who we are and what our experiences are and will be. One of my daily practices is reading the Bible. I have noticed how many of its characters are named from circumstances in which they were born.

In certain countries of Africa, people are named based on the day they were born, their familial placement, or their gender. Other traditions name a child based on parental personality traits and conditions surrounding their birth. People's names bear their history. My name is a reminder of the circumstances in which I was born and the wish Papa had for me.

I am amused to hear people's comments when they first meet me. "Pollyanna? I've never met a Pollyanna before."

"Wow. What a beautiful name!"

"There's a movie titled *Pollyanna*. Did your parents name you after the movie character? Are you a Pollyanna?"

My response usually is, "Yes, I am in the flesh."

When my friends speak of me, they say things like: "There is always some excitement in Polly's life. She is always joyful! You'll never know when something is wrong in her life because she is always so positive. Even when things go wrong, she still smiles. I don't know how she does it. She always offers a brighter perspective on every situation."

One of my sisters recently told me, "One constant thing about you is that you are never depressed."

It's true. There are so many reasons why I should be glad. I focus on those things. The negative things in life will always be there. I address them as they come. If I can handle them, I am elated. If I can't, I let them go and hand them over to God. He will handle them for me. Papa told me on numerous occasions that he was happy that I turned out to be the person he envisioned me to be. I am content that he had the satisfaction to see his wish fulfilled. And so, "The Glad Game" continues.

TWO

PLAYING THE GAME

Based on Maman, Papa's wish for me came true: playing "The Glad Game" became an expression of who I was. When I faced challenges, I naturally looked for the good and didn't allow negative circumstances to effect my optimistic nature. So it was no surprise that at challenging times in my life, I would play the game.

When my mother said to me on my thirtieth birthday, "Look how God is blessing you now!" she was referring to my days of affluence. Life was so different then. My husband, Baldwin, was a successful businessman who traveled the world for his company while I stayed home to care for our three small children. We lived in a beautiful three-bedroom condo, and we traveled constantly and enjoyed "the good life." Baldwin used to (and still does) love to say, "Life is good! And it doesn't get much better than this!"

Maman had no way of knowing that one year after our conversation on my birthday our circumstances would radically change and my optimistic nature would be put to its most arduous test. We lost everything! The company for which Baldwin was working went bankrupt. When our savings were depleted, we had to count our losses and sell some of our possessions because we could no longer afford to keep them. As hard as things were, we had difficulty parting with some of them. We drove two brand new Jaguars. My jet-black Vanden Plas XJ6 was lined with crème leather interior, while Baldwin's silver-gray XJS had sleek black leather interior.

Our biggest challenge came when we had to return the Jags to the dealer. I loved my Jag and couldn't imagine driving anything else. However, we had no other choice. If we didn't return it, sooner or later they would be repossessed, and we could not allow that to happen. I told Baldwin that I needed some time to reprogram my mind before I faced the inevitable. Papa had told me, "Your mindset determines how you handle situations in life." Well, this was the time for me to work on my mindset because I was not ready.

A few days later I woke up and calmly said to Baldwin, "I'm ready. Let's do it today." During that period of our life, Tommy and Sandra were our closest friends and business colleagues. We spent an inordinate amount of wonderful time together. We called them and shared our plans with them. They sympathized with us and offered to take us back home from the car dealership. The four of us had ridden in the Jags many times before, and it was only fitting that we be together for our last ride.

Inside the car rain clouds flooded my father's "glad game" with teardrops. In perfect irony, outside the bright July sun beamed down on our parade to the dealership. The cloudless sky swallowed me into its beauty like an endless blue abyss. This view reminded me of the phrase, "the sky is the limit to what I can have." I thought of this phrase as I drove the Jag on that day. It seemed as if the earth was rejoicing in my misery. I may have borne the situation better if the weather had been bleak and gloomy, matching my mood. Instead, I was left to suffer my heartache with silent tears.

Every sound in the car was magnified! The engine seemed unbearably loud, where it had purred before. The shock of going over the bumps reminded me of moments spent on roller coaster rides. The only difference was that I was driving in a comfortable, luxurious Jaguar. What a paradox! Baldwin was in his car; I was in mine. Tommy and Sandra followed us in their new Cadillac Seville. It felt as though we were in a funeral procession about to bury a loved one. My heart beat loudly in my chest as my thoughts danced from topic to topic—transportation, money, survival, comfort, facing people. I found it hard to settle on one. The short moment between getting out of the car and turning the keys over to the dealer seemed endless.

Baldwin returned the keys while I joined my friends and waited in their car. Since Baldwin had called ahead to announce his arrival at the dealership, the manager was expecting him. The gentleman greeted Baldwin at the door with a long face, talking as though he was presenting his condolences. He led Baldwin to his office. They stayed there briefly. Then I saw them reappear. Some salesmen approached Baldwin to present their sympathies for the turn of events with the company. Baldwin reported that the manager told him as he was leaving, "Don't worry man; you'll be back here to get a new Jag before you know it." They patted his shoulders as they bid him farewell. Baldwin left with a renewed determination that he would return—soon.

Not a word was uttered during the first fifteen minutes of the ride back home. I finally broke the silence and began to play "The Glad Game." I proceeded to recount the various places we had traveled together in the Jags. We drove to resorts in Wisconsin on several occasions, went to banquets and restaurants, attended numerous business meetings, and engaged in fun times together. We reminisced on the time when Jena's daughter, Brenda, (mutual friends) was graduating from high school. She requested to ride in my Jag instead of a rented limousine. Baldwin waxed and shined the Jag, put on a black suit, a chauffeur's cap and white gloves, and picked up Brenda and chauffeured her to the event. Baldwin opened the door to help her out of the car. Her friends were there watching. He said to her, "Shall I wait for you Miss.?"

Brenda responded, "Yes, of course." He waited for her in front of the hotel until she reappeared at the end of the function.

We laughed as Baldwin described the facial expressions of Brenda's classmates. With dropped jaws they queried, "You have a chauffeur? Wow! You're rich!" Brenda turned and winked at Baldwin as she walked away into the hotel. Priceless!

As we reminisced on these memorable moments, I commented, "Do you know how many people only fantasize about these things? We actually experienced them. We ought to consider ourselves blessed!" Our spirit was lifted, and we resolved that this challenge we were experiencing was temporary, and we would soon be back on top. We all felt better, hopeful, embracing the future with open arms.

Upon our return home, we had to figure out how to get around without a car. We lived in a western suburb of Chicago, Illinois, and our home was a distance away from our church, our friends, and our business associates. Our children were small; the youngest was two months old. We were certainly in a predicament with no solution in sight.

When my brother, Jean, had moved to the Chicago area with his family two years earlier, he had parked one of his cars in our condo's parking garage. I remember complaining about it several times to Baldwin, saying, "Why did Jean have to leave this jalopy here? This is embarrassing. I don't want people to see this car and associate it with us. Get rid of it."

I repeatedly commented that it was a shame to have that car around, and I got angry every time my eyes fell on it. To say that it looked terrible was an understatement. The car was dilapidated. It seemed that the more I insisted that the car be removed the less affected Baldwin was, because it remained in the same space for two years.

Let me paint a picture of this car for you. It was a fifteen year old, two-door Toyota Corolla. Having lived through rain, snow, and sleet for years, the car featured a few patches of its original blue while the rest had faded beyond recognition or been replaced by rust. The car resembled a giant piece of Swiss cheese. The car leaked when it rained. The leather seats were torn. The stereo and temperature systems had stopped functioning. The mileage was over 250,000, and all the tires had been bald and flat for months. There were holes everywhere—from the ceiling, to the sides, and even inside the car. The biggest hole was in the floor on the passenger's side, and it was covered with a thick piece of cardboard. Surely the only thing that could lay claim to the car was a demolition truck because it was past ready to be recycled. I never asked Jean why he kept that car.

While assessing our options, Baldwin pointed out, "We have too many debts to add a new one to the pile. After all, no one will sell us a car unless we pay cash. Polly, we cannot afford to buy a car now, new or old." Then, to my great horror, he remembered Jean's car. Baldwin said, "Let's take a look at the car Jean abandoned."

"Oh no! There has to be another way. Not that car! Lord, this is a nightmare!" I responded, mortified.

As Baldwin sometimes does, he ignored me and proceeded to investigate the jalopy. I refused to look while he examined it. I was torn; although part of me hoped that the car wouldn't start, the other part prayed that it would. I felt stuck and I hated it. Then I turned and watched with mixed emotions as Baldwin resurrected the car from the dead. From that day on, we drove Old Blue, as we named her.

It didn't take me long to accept Old Blue as our only mode of transportation. As soon as we repaired her tires and cleaned her, we tried her out on the road. The first good thing out of this situation was that the maximum speed that Old Blue could reach was 55 mph, no matter how low the accelerator pedal was pressed. It at least afforded me the peace of mind that I longed for when riding in the Jags with Baldwin.

You see, Baldwin was always racing in and out of traffic. His average speed was 80 mph, and it was not unusual for him to drive more than 100 mph on the highway. There were times I thought my heart would stop beating from anxiety. I blessed Old Blue for her maximum speed of 55 mph.

As with the Jags, we had many adventures in Old Blue. The first of these adventures happened that same evening. The five of us—Baldwin, our three children, and I—got in the car and drove to an evangelistic series we attended during the summer on the south side of Chicago. We had not missed one session, and we were not about to be discouraged by our circumstances.

Everyone was there. Cars were parked around the tent, and patrols were directing traffic and parking. Prior to that day, when we entered the driveway, we were quickly ushered to our reserved area. Our beautiful black Jaguar was parked in its rightful place, next to the evangelist's red and white Cadillac. The Jag was the patrols' favorite, so they made sure that it was stationed in the most secure place of honor.

That evening we arrived at the gate driving Old Blue. Without looking at us, the guard motioned for us to park in another section of the lot. As we started to drive past him, our eyes met and he recognized us. I cringed with embarrassment, wishing I could hide under the seat. His eyes widened, and the creases in his forehead registered his shock. He whistled loudly; then he paused for a moment to verify that his imagination was not getting the best of him. Baldwin and I forced a smile. He looked at us again then pointed at the car. We nodded. Without saying another word, he motioned us to our usual place.

Later on he spoke to Baldwin and found out that we had lost the Jag. He was empathetic. In spite of our new state of affairs, the security guard reserved that special place for Old Blue for the duration of the series. The good: there were still some people who valued us more than our material things and were willing to preserve our dignity. God bless him.

We also drove our friend, Martha Burt, home at the end of each meeting. Given our new situation, we thought it best to have someone else take her. As she always did, Martha met us at the car at the end of the meeting. When she came to Old Blue she exclaimed, "Where is my Jag?"

"There is no more Jag," I told her, unsure of what her reaction would be.

"My God, you lost our beautiful Jag, too? Oh no!" She responded.

"Baldwin found you another ride home." I continued.

I'll never forget what Martha said, "What's wrong with this one? If it's good enough for you, it's good enough for me. We rode together in luxury; we'll ride together in poverty. We're friends, girl! Take me home."

Martha got in the car and looked at us, "Waiting for somebody else?" We quickly followed—the children and I in the back, Baldwin and Martha in the front—and we drove off. I was deeply moved by this act of friendship and support. I was happy to be in the back because neither Baldwin nor Martha could see my tears. I thanked her on several occasions for the gift of her friendship.

What a friend! I thought. *How blessed I am to have her in my life.*

Martha and other friends demonstrated to me that friendship does not depend on material possessions but on the commitment we make to each other. As the old adage appropriately says, "You know who your friends are when the chips are down." We were poor materially, but wealthy in friends.

൹   ൹   ൹

We thought things couldn't get any worse, but we were sadly mistaken. Two weeks after we repaired Old Blue, we got into an accident. Old Blue was hit from the back and damaged. We were not physically hurt, but emotionally, we were devastated. Scared and confused, we wondered in disbelief at what was happening to our life. To add to its long list of defects, Old Blue now had a big dent adorning its tail end. The driver's seat became dislocated and could no longer sustain itself. We used a rope to secure the seat in place and put the spare tire behind it to keep it upright.

I distinctly remember the Chicagoland Adventist Youth Federation Year-end banquet at McCormick Place. As vice president of the Federation, it was my responsibility to organize the banquet, and since I organized it, I had to attend. We drove to the opulent place in Old Blue, and valet parking was the only option. There was no way I was going to walk a few blocks in my three-inch heels just to save face, so we waited for the valet.

When the attendant approached the car, we were amused as his jaw dropped. Baldwin stepped out of Old Blue dressed in his black tuxedo, covered by his long black coat. He came around the car to open the door for me. The attendant's jaw dropped further when I stepped out draped in my full-length black mink coat, wearing an elegant and expensive silk dress. Baldwin smiled and gave him the car key. The young man repeatedly looked at us then at the car. I could only imagine what he was thinking. Our smile widened. The attendant reluctantly entered the car and had difficulty changing the gears as he drove away. We were the recipients of this and similar reactions several times throughout the year.

Some people must have thought that we were playing a prank on them.

Papa used to say to me, "Whatever challenge you experience in life, remember that it will last for only a moment. The way you interact with the situation will determine the quality of your experience. Just remember, this too shall pass."

Looking at us, no one would have known that we were going through a financial hurricane. Even our relatives and friends didn't realize the full extent of our situation because nothing about us reflected our reality. Since we didn't sell our clothes (except for my fur), we were always impeccably dressed. When we went to church and other free functions, I maintained my smile and cheerfulness, and continued to encourage others. I refused to allow my circumstances to alter who I was. I continued to remain fully engaged in life as before. Papa always said to me, "Be content with what you have, and in everything give thanks."

During this difficult time, I kept looking to our children. I must say that throughout this period our children were our greatest blessing and comfort. I daily thanked God for them. They were not concerned about their dwelling place, the clothes they wore, or the kinds of food they ate. As long as they were with us, they were happy and secure. Children are precious jewels; if only we could learn to be like them, life would be so much simpler and happier.

We continued to travel to various places in Old Blue for almost a year. We created numerous and priceless memories. Unfortunately, she stopped working one day as we were driving, never to be resurrected again. Old Blue was finally laid to rest. She was towed away and must have been recycled or found her permanent home in a junkyard. She had served her purpose.

I remember waking up the morning after Old Blue's death, dialoguing internally, *Pollyanna, challenges come for a reason and a season. When you encounter them, look for the lessons to be learned. Every challenge is an opportunity for growth and strength, and as you go through them, keep in mind what your father told you, "This too shall pass." When tough situations arise, look forward to the person you will have become when you get to the other side.*

I often say, "Lord, just help me understand the lesson so I can grow through this situation quickly." We can find the good in every situation.

THREE

TRADITIONS AND RITUALS

Our parents continued to practice some traditions and rituals in our home even after we left Haiti. Although they assimilated the American cultures of the U.S. and Canada, they ingrained in us certain practices that kept us connected to God and our native land. For spiritual growth, we engaged in daily worship rituals; for nurturing one another, we celebrated birthdays; and for patriotic connection, we observed New Year's Day traditions.

Prayer and worship have always been important aspects of my life. Growing up in a pastor's home, we founded every daily exercise in praise to God; prayer was the most integral part of our home. We prayed for every occasion, good or bad. We prayed for blessings before punishment; we prayed in the car before we would travel; we prayed at the dining table, and of course, before going to bed at night.

As long as I can remember, we had worship every day, morning and night. My siblings and I awoke at six o'clock in the morning to the sound of Papa playing the piano. He would play a few songs, allowing us enough time to get up and wash before worship. I can recall the last song ("Lord in the Morning Thou Shall

Hear") he always played to signal that worship was about to begin, and we had better be in our seats when the last note of that song was played.

When I was very young, we had worship three times a day: morning, noon, and night. Daily worship was solemn in my home. Papa would lead us in song service, and, in an effort to encourage us to join in, Maman would cheerfully sing along. Imagine nine sleepy children holding a songbook trying to sing at six o'clock in the morning. Each of us had an individual Bible and hymnal from which we read and sang. After singing we read one or two chapters together from the Bible. Then we would study the children's lesson, and Maman would read the adult Sabbath School lesson while Papa would answer the questions from the lesson.

My parents wanted us to be more involved, but we were more interested in sleep than worship. However, we were more involved in evening worships. We learned memory verses and psalms. We would sing a couple more songs and some of us would pray, including Maman. Then, my father would close the session with prayer. When Papa prayed I felt transported to heaven. I believed that surely his prayers would be answered. I wanted to pray like Papa. After prayer we got up and followed the custom of wishing each other well, "Bonne Journée!" (Have a good day!), with an embrace and kiss. When guests were visiting our home, they were invited to join us in worship. In the U.S. and Canada, guests were always pleasantly surprised at this practice.

My favorite worship time was Friday evenings when we opened the Sabbath. I enjoyed harmonizing in the songs I sang with my parents and siblings. After worship we would have a wonderful meal, and my siblings and I would talk and sing for hours.

As I got older, the worship experience became more and more unpleasant for me. I didn't enjoy waking up so early just to have family worship. My father was always concerned that we weren't developing a close relationship with Jesus. He didn't think that we spent sufficient time on our knees praying and reading our Bibles. He thought that we depended on him to get through to God. He was accurate; we relied on his relationship with God to receive guidance and blessings. I felt forced to worship. It could last about an hour or more. It's not that I had a problem with worship in general or with any particular element. I enjoyed singing and praying; I learned a lot from the readings; and being together as a family was a wonderful experience. The issue for me was that I just did not want to get up at six o'clock every morning. I couldn't wait to leave home so that I could sleep in as late as I wanted to.

The opportunity to leave home came when I went to Andrews University my sophomore year of college. However, I did not find myself sleeping in. Instead, I was amazed to find myself studying and praying at six o'clock in the morning, pausing at noon for a short prayer, and having worship again before I went to sleep. Shocking! Daily worship was my parent's religious ritual and expectation of us. When I was finally on my own, I felt the need to develop my own relationship with God. But I couldn't stop the worship ritual because, unknowingly, it had become a part of me.

During my years in college, I had the opportunity to get to know God for myself and develop a relationship with Him. I could no longer rely on my parents' faith; I had to develop my own. I had a head start though: I had my parents' example. They had and still have a strong faith. I admired my father's faith and strong relationship with God. So, I sought to develop my own relationship with God through continuous prayer and daily worship at six o'clock in the morning. God and I, we were profoundly related at Andrews University.

Around that time I began a relationship with Baldwin. In sharing our childhood memories, we realized that we had so much in common. Our childhood family worship experiences were remarkably similar. It's like going into a McDonald's restaurant in Tokyo, Japan, and having the person at the counter greet you exactly like they greet you here in the U.S.—"Hello, welcome to

McDonald's. May I help you?"—with the same cheerful smile and direct eye contact. The technique for starting worship in his home was the same as mine—the piano began playing at six o'clock every morning. Our parents must have gone to the same family worship school. Of course, when I was growing up, worship was a ritual: the same time, the same songs, and the same type of readings—the children's and adult Sabbath School lessons—the same prayers.

But when Baldwin and I started having worship together, the worship never felt mundane. In the mornings, around six o'clock, we prayed together, and in the evenings, around 9:30 p.m., we would meet in the visiting room at the women's dorm and have worship. Miss Friestad, the women's dean, would chase male visitors out of the dorm, but somehow she allowed us to stay in that room sometimes past visiting hours to finish our worship.

Those prayer times together were definitely bonding experiences for us. We got to be with each other. Nothing seemed repetitive, boring, or routine about those sessions. They were thrilling, invigorating. We sang, we read, we prayed. These were the same things we used to do at home in family worship, but somehow it was all different. It was voluntary, and I was with the one I loved. During these times I felt free to be myself. Our prayers were open, honest, and nurturing of each other.

The bonds between my family, my husband, and me that were created during our worship sessions can never be broken. When we married and had children, Baldwin and I set up our own worship traditions. After disagreeing on whether or not to maintain the same rituals we had growing up, we decided instead to hold worship a little later in the morning with a simple prayer instead of a "full-blown" worship. When my children were born, I had worship two to three times a day.

As they grew older and went to school, the number lessened, but I make sure that this tradition continues, because daily worship is valuable to spiritual formation and maintenance. Before we pray together during evening worship, each person shares blessings of the day as well as concerns, and we all pray for each other. I want prayer to be fundamental in my children's lives. I want to pass on this heritage of a relationship with Christ, formed through daily worship and prayer, to my children just as Papa did for me.

The difference between my childhood worship experiences and those of my children is that we have implemented various interactive and intergenerational strategies in our worship sessions with them. I am convinced that worship is very important. It is important for me individually and for my relationship with Baldwin and with my children. I realize that most of the things I know about God I learned in worship as a child. The lesson I learned from this experience is that, as parents, we must set standards and rituals for our children. We need to teach our children about God for their own spiritual and moral formation. With consistent repetition, these practices will become a natural expression of themselves.

Through family worship Papa taught us to develop and enhance our own personal relationship with God and to take time out from our busy life to reconnect with God. I learned that access to the voice of God is found in moments of quietude. If it weren't for my personal prayer life and seeking after God, I would not have been able to hear Him leading me along the way.

I appreciate this quote from Ellen G. White: "All who are under the training of God need the quiet hour for communication with their own hearts, with nature and with God. . . . When every other voice is hushed, and in quietness we wait before Him, the silence of soul makes more distinct the voice of God" (*Ministry of Healing,* p. 58). Family worship taught me to personally connect with God, to refocus, and to "be still and know that I am [He is] God" (Psalm 46:10, NIV).

の　の　の

Birthdays were special days in my home; my parents made sure of it. My mother prepared our favorite meals, and dinnertime always ended with a big birthday cake and ice cream. As a rule, dessert was not a course included in our daily meals. Maman strongly believed that excess sugar was not healthy for us, so she did not serve it, except on our birthdays. Since there were so many of us children, there were birthdays spread throughout the year, and we looked forward to each one. The month of April was very special to the family because that's when all the men were born: Papa and my two brothers. Along with their birthdays, April was my parents' wedding anniversary and Papa's ordination as a minister of the gospel. We looked forward to each other's birthdays as if they were our own—we relished any chance to celebrate with dessert.

We rarely received material birthday gifts—the birthday blessing was the gift. The blessing made our birthdays so special! A typical birthday began with family worship. We sang the celebrant's favorite songs, and he/she read the scripture of the day. Before prayer, Papa would ask the birthday person to share his/her greatest wish for the coming year, then he would have the celebrant kneel down next to him. He would then lay his hand on his/her head and pray the prayer of blessing.

The prayer of blessing included praise to God for giving the family the gift of his/her birth, praise for the blessings from the past and present, forgiveness of his/her sins, rededication of his/her life as a gift to God, a request for his/her wish and specific needs, and finally, a declaration of bountiful blessings and success on him/her for the upcoming year. On this day, we recommitted our lives to God and started all over again with Him. The prayer was so powerful! We were sure that God would favorably answer Papa's prayer; we could take it to the bank. When I got up from my knees, I was always certain that every word Papa had uttered would come to fruition during the coming year.

The birthday blessing set the tone for the whole year. Without the blessing, it seemed as though our birthdays would have been meaningless. When we grew up and left home, Papa called us to give us our blessing over the phone. It was just as powerful to us as it was in person. I felt blessed. My faith was profound, believing that the year was going to be extraordinary, just as he would pray.

My brothers and sisters' reactions were similar. We felt empowered, special, and ecstatic. He talked about us positively, expounded on our qualities and gifts, and predicted how we would impact the world. He would present possibilities for us in such a way that I was amazed at what he saw in my siblings and me. When he talked about me, I would say to myself, "Who me?" But if Papa said it, I believed it. On our birthdays, my father would declare our future, and we expected it to materialize. Some declarations did come true, while others did not. Not for lack of his faith, but maybe for ours.

After worship and the blessing, everyone embraced the birthday celebrant. We then proceeded to the dining room for breakfast where the birthday feasts began. We had a great breakfast and lunch, but dinner topped them all. It was the best meal of the year. We all dressed up, and the birthday boy or girl wore his or her favorite attire. Maman would make the girls' hairdo special on that day. The birthday person sat in Maman's seat across from Papa, at the head of the table. Maman served the meal in six or seven courses, and we all displayed our best dining etiquette.

Papa proceeded to share the birthday person's story while we ate. He gave detailed information about our birth, what we looked like as newborns, and where we lived. He shared special incidents that happened to or because of us. He repeated the silly and funny things we said and did and even sang our favorite songs, mimicking the way we said the words as toddlers. We loved hearing stories about ourselves—it didn't matter how many times we had heard them before. Every year there was an addition to the story, marking our growth from the previous year. The feast ended with the presentation of the birthday cake. The cake was served with ice cream and garnished with some type of fruit. When they could afford it, my parents gave us a gift, which was a great surprise since we never expected it. We didn't have birthday parties where friends were invited. A birthday was always a private family affair.

My parents made our birthdays a truly special day. Papa repeated this same exercise every year without fail. We were all so happy, surrounded by much laughter. Being part of a large family tends to make one feel invisible sometimes. There are so many children to take care of and think of everyone cannot always get all the attention that he/she wants or thinks they deserve. But on our birthdays we were the focus. All eyes were fixed on us. We felt like the center of the universe for a day.

In Haiti New Year's Day is Independence Day. It is considered to be the biggest day of celebration. The festivities begin before Christmas and continue through New Year's Day. The practices remind me of the Kwanza celebration among African-Americans here in the states. We really didn't celebrate Christmas. We never had a Christmas tree. We never gave or received presents for Christmas. Although it was practiced by others around us, we never seemed to miss it. That's how it always was. Even when we came to the states and Canada, we continued to live as before.

I realize that we didn't miss the Christmas celebration so much because of the New Year's Day celebration. We spent sleepless nights anticipating the festivities of the New Year. On New Year's Eve we would have prayer meeting, then eat and drink eggnog. The next morning we would wake up early. We'd have worship, and Papa would make a wish and bless each of us for the year. We then had breakfast, which was a traditional butternut squash soup with bread.

Then we would go visit our grandparents, relatives, and neighbors and wish them a happy New Year. It was a big thing for all of the children in the neighborhood, for it was the custom around the country. The elders would bless us and give us gifts. We went from house to house, paying our respects and receiving good wishes and gifts. That was the greatest event of the year for us. We collected many, many gifts. Though we were tired when we got home, we were excited about opening our presents. That was the only time during the year when we were certain to receive toys. New Year's Day was like Thanksgiving, Christmas, and Halloween altogether.

Interestingly, when I had my own family, I continued what was familiar to me. I did not celebrate Christmas, and since my husband never celebrated Christmas, it didn't matter to him. Friends scolded me for not following the general customs of my surroundings. They felt that my poor little children would suffer trauma from being deprived of the pleasure of believing in Santa Claus and practicing the rituals of Christmas. It would come back to hurt me, they said; I was called a Scrooge many times.

The point is that I enjoy the Christmas colors and look forward to listening to carols. I love to drive around and admire the beautifully decorated homes and businesses. I love the spirit that surrounds the Christmas season. It would be great if this spirit were exhibited throughout the year. Really, why not have the spirit of gratitude and love all year long? I have nothing against the activities surrounding Christmas; I just don't celebrate it as others do. But I celebrate New Years' Day.

When my children were older, I decided to buy a Christmas tree and decorate it. This action was a result of my daughter's insistence on me buying one. She had helped my girlfriend Joy decorate her tree, but that wasn't enough. She wanted one of her own, so I conceded. My sisters and I bought the tree and trimmings, and my younger sisters helped my daughter, Gabrielle, decorate it. They made a ceremony of it. For this was their first Christmas tree, too. They sang Christmas carols as they decorated it. When they finished, they prepared hot chocolate to drink as they sat around admiring their creation. They were all excited about it. Maybe they too may have felt deprived all those years.

My sons, on the other hand, had no interest in the Christmas festivities and didn't participate. They said to me, "Mom, I thought we didn't celebrate Christmas!" They were also resentful when they and their father were expected to dispose of the tree at the end of the festive season. They said that if Gabrielle and I made it a ritual, *we* needed to make arrangements to have it removed in the future. The following year, my daughter showed no interest, and the issue of a Christmas tree was never raised again. I guess her curiosity was satisfied.

Again, on New Year's Day, dinner was a grand affair. Guests were invited, and we had a great meal. We had great times together. The festivities continued on the second day of January as well. New Year's Day dinner is somewhat like Thanksgiving dinner in the U.S. As I was growing up, after dinner we would gather together and Papa would make a speech. Then, we would open our gifts. Since moving to the U.S. and Canada, we continued the same custom. Instead of visiting the elders, we make phone calls. Even after leaving home, we gather together for New Year's Day. Instead of receiving gifts from the elders, we, the siblings, exchange gifts with each other and give presents to our nephews and nieces. The tradition of the New Year's Day celebration was meaningful to Papa, and it remains a family tradition.

Traditions and rituals are good for us. They establish who we are. They maintain longevity. We pass on our heritage, beliefs, and passion through traditions and rituals. They create a sense of belonging, lasting relationships, and pride. Traditions and rituals create memories we keep for a lifetime. They provide us a heritage we're proud of and can pass on to future generations. Traditions and rituals keep us alive because it is the sharing of who we are that gives us immortality. I thank my parents for passing these on to us. We will always keep them alive.

FOUR

SIBLINGS = FRIENDS

Papa taught us the importance of family. He told us that, "The most valuable commodity that you possess is your siblings, your family. Learn to trust, support, and rely on each other under all circumstances." Through the years we endured challenges and celebrations. We were together through it all, and our experiences together created a bond that will never be severed. As adults, Papa would observe how we interacted with each other, and he would frequently say with a smile, "I can die now because my work is complete. My family is strong, and I know that you will support each other." My father was satisfied that his goal was accomplished in the lives of his children.

Papa instilled in us virtues that he thought were vital to the existence of a family. We were to protect each other: if anyone touched one of us, they touched all of us. We didn't go to many places, but we could be sure that all of our outings and interactions would always occur in the presence of a family member. We all were thrown together without a choice.

As a child, I was the shadow of my older sister Rosie. I was placed beside Rosie as her companion. We became inseparable since we rarely went anywhere without the other. We became best friends. Papa wanted his children to be taught about the Lord and to attend Seventh-day Adventist schools to reinforce our religious beliefs and practices. However, when we were in the primary grades, we were sent to a Catholic school because there were no Adventist church schools in town. The closest school was hours away. My father made an agreement with the nuns that we would not study the catechism or any Catholic literature; we were exempt from going to mass or any religious activity.

On Wednesdays, the whole school went to mass at the nearby cathedral. Rosie and I were the only two students left in the whole school. We had to remain in class to do assigned work during that time. We hated staying there by ourselves. It felt as though we were punished for having differing religious views. These Wednesdays drew us closer to each other. Fortunately, by mid-year, Papa moved us to another town where there was a church school.

The following year we were sent to a boarding school to ensure that we received an Adventist education. We were placed in a dormitory with grown female students. Our room was adjacent to the dean's apartment, who was our surrogate nanny and responsible for our care. She did the best she could, but sometimes she punished us severely, whipping us undeservedly.

One day the dean was upset at Rosie for something she had done, so the dean hit Rosie on the head with a pail while she was in the shower. I don't remember what Rosie did, but she didn't deserve such an extreme response. On my birthday, I got three spankings. One of the spankings was because my socks were not as dry as she expected. The dean spanked me for not having washed the socks sooner and had me wear them wet to a Christmas party. The next evening, she had friends over for a party. We were not invited. All the lights in the dorm were switched off because all the adult students had gone home for the holidays. Rosie and I spent the evening in the dark, sitting and crying together on a bench. We looked forward to the next morning when Papa would come to take us home for the holidays.

When Papa found out about the misery we had been enduring, he decided that we would not return to that school. Instead, he took us to another church school, where we resided with relatives. Papa truly believed in Christian education. Unfortunately, our relatives didn't treat us any better than the dean. Although my father paid adequately for our care, we were not properly fed; everyone else was fed first, and we were given the leftover crumbs. We were mistreated and ostracized.

When we shared our plight with our maternal grandmother who lived in another town, she was indignant and began sending us food at school every day. She waited until the end of the year to tell my mother, at which point Maman became enraged and told Papa to bring her children back to her. She was confident that she could take care of her own children and was not about to allow other people to mistreat us. The following year Papa was moved to a city that had a church school, and our family was finally together again.

A few years later, my parents began making plans to send us to France to complete our education. But the plans changed before we left. Instead, Papa sent us to the United States. He told us that "there were endless opportunities" for us in the U.S., so Rosie and I were put on a plane headed to New York. A new life away from our family was about to begin. Rosie worked, and I went to school. As young teenagers, it was difficult being away from home, unable to speak or understand English, and uncertain about our future.

Rosie used to sleepwalk. Sometimes in the middle of the night, Rosie would sit on the fire escape stairs, even when it was freezing. When I realized that she was sleepwalking, I would try to stay awake at night to watch her. But I didn't succeed at keeping her inside most of the times. Every time I found her, she was sitting in the same spot just staring. When the family reunited, she never sleepwalked again. I found out later that it was a manifestation of psychological disturbance because of her separation from her family.

There were times when I was very anxious and concerned about our future. But being a Pollyanna, I looked for the good in everything I did. I anticipated every good thing that would happen, and I survived. Really, I didn't have major issues because my big sister made sure that I was taken care of. Rosie was my companion and my closest friend. We cried together, laughed together, and prayed together. We were inseparable. We supported each other through those experiences and grew stronger and stronger. To this day, Rosie and I share a special bond that is unique to only us. When we retire, we plan to build our houses next to each other and grow old together.

My parents were very strict. They taught Rosie and me lessons in hopes that we would learn well and pass them on to our younger siblings. When I was young, Papa told Rosie and me, "Because you are the oldest you are to set the example for your younger brothers and sisters. Be mindful of how you behave around them because what you do will impact them positively or negatively as they will follow what you do. You are the example."

I considered these words as a life sentence. I didn't feel that it was a privilege to be older. There were so many things that we were obligated to do as well as forbidden from doing that it seemed like a burden to be the oldest, responsible for the younger siblings. I had to be careful that my words and actions would not influence them adversely. Given that my family was very spiritual, it also felt as though my siblings' salvation depended on us. We had to be careful not to influence them to go down a path to hell. Although that wasn't Papa's intention, I interpreted it that way.

This concept of being an example pervaded my life. Not only did my parents expect me to be an example at home, but as a pastor's kid, I was expected to be an example in the church as well. Church members had high expectations of us. We went to church school, and everyone knew who Papa was. I couldn't be invisible anywhere because there was no place to hide to be my authentic self. The pressure of constant scrutiny from everyone at home, in church, and in school was agonizing. They expected us to be "perfect," and there was no room for mistakes. I was the reflection of everybody's expectations. It felt like I was living in a glass house.

I wasn't sure who I was outside of being "the example." But luckily, I got a break, and things began to change. The evolution of the new "me" began when Maman, Rosie, and I moved to Boston, Massachusetts. For two and half years, we had no younger siblings to model for—it was just the three of us and Papa when he visited on breaks from Lincoln, Nebraska, where he was a full-time student at the time.

The members of the church we were attending had a different attitude toward us: they treated us like the other young people. We did not need to be more perfect than them; the church members had the same expectations for all of us. When we became active, they were genuinely supportive of us. It was then that I noticed a difference in me: I felt less pressured.

While the stigma of being a pastor's kid, especially Pastor Naasson Proper's daughter, has followed me all my life, I learned to flourish as an individual during our time in Boston. Rosie and I were finally free to be ourselves. As we matured into our new, free characters, we were still the best of friends.

ᆽᢒ   ᆽᢒ   ᆽᢒ

Rosie and my other siblings are one of the greatest gifts my parents gave me. They are invaluable treasures. My parents had eleven children altogether, but they lost two daughters along the way. Having six sisters and two brothers as friends and keeping these friendships healthy is challenging. With nine personalities, one can easily feel overwhelmed and alone in the crowd. At the same time, siblings can be great friends. We talk to each other all the time about everything, and regardless of the situation, my siblings' love and support are constant.

ﻌ   ﻌ   ﻌ

Whenever the family gathered together, we could rest assured that someone would start trouble. In an attempt to diffuse the fire, Maman or Papa would advise us not to take the other seriously. We didn't always listen though. When we got mad and responded, things sometimes became very heated. But one great thing I admired about my siblings and me is that we never held grudges against each other. We were able to quickly let go of things.

Papa was happy that his children were so bonded. He felt blessed to have sons and daughters who were close. He was assured that we would remain true to each other and take care of each other just as he raised us to. I love having so many sisters. Along with my brothers, they are my gifts from Papa and Maman, and I treasure them all. When we are together, wherever we are is home, just the way Papa wanted.

FIVE

OTHERS MAY, BUT YOU CANNOT

The phrase "Others may, but *you* cannot" represented Papa's standard of behavior and excellence both for himself and his family. It was Papa's way of saying, "You don't live by others' standards, but by God's and mine." This phrase may have been intended to be motivating, but I didn't like to hear him utter it. I felt it was unfair for him to deprive us of being involved in so many activities while growing up. Everyone else was doing it. Everybody would be there. If others could, why couldn't we? We were no different than they were. But Papa had his standards set for the family, and no one could change them.

Papa's high expectations often seemed unattainable. As I grew older, he found new ways to instill in us his idea of standards: "Our standards are not dictated by men," or "You cannot do something because others are doing it." In one of our debates, he said to me, "Ma fille, your actions have to be determined by God's standards, not by men. Before you act you must ask yourself, 'Is this according to God's will or men's?' If it is not according to God, then don't do it. Do not follow the crowd if their philosophies and beliefs are contrary to God's (yours). You must have the courage to stand alone if you must."

"But people will think that we are strange. They will laugh at us."

"I know it's hard to do. Believe me, I am speaking from experience. But when you stand on your convictions, you will gain the respect of others. Jesus did it. You can do it too."

Papa's standards for his family were built on honor, integrity, honesty, courage, and excellence. He was committed in instilling these qualities in us because, as he put it, "they are the traits of a man or a woman of character."

When it came to honor, my father was relentless. He taught us to honor God and honor our family name. That's who we were, Christian and Prosper. He reminded us that we were children of God and we needed to honor Him in everything we did. He would tell us, "People ought to know that you are Christians by the way you speak and act. You cannot take it lightly."

Both my parents instilled biblical and universal principles in us. They used every opportunity to teach us lessons about God. I remember as a little girl when my siblings and I would quarrel, Maman would call us and say, "You must not have anything to do, that's why you are getting yourselves in trouble. Each of you go get your Bible and sit in that corner (she placed each of us in a separate place), and memorize a particular psalm or passage. Don't get up until you know it. Then come recite it to me." We would reluctantly obey, going to our assigned corner and memorizing the psalms. A great number of the psalms I know today were learned that way.

Then there was the Prosper name we were never to forget. We were to honor the family name and uphold it wherever we went. Honor and preserving our family name seemed to be more important to Papa than life. In fact, he seemed to be unreasonable in that regard. As Proverbs 22:1 says, "A good name is more desirable than great riches; to be esteemed is better than silver or gold" (NIV). This rang true for him.

Interestingly, we were judged by higher standards by people outside of our home as well. If our behavior was inappropriate in public, we were called on it, "Aren't you Pastor Prosper's son-daughter?" or "You can't do that; you are Pastor Prosper's child!" We were judged by higher standards than others. Papa used to say that "with privilege comes responsibility."

When I was twenty-one years old, I worked as an intern during the summer in Montreal, Canada. Papa was the speaker of an evangelistic series in that city, and I was an intern on his team. I was assigned a partner who was lodged in our home. Fortunately, she happened to be a childhood friend. Every morning Papa met with his team for prayer, planning, and training. Usually, I went home for lunch with him. As time progressed, my partner and I had lunch together, and I didn't go home every day. One day Papa heard that one of the young men in the team invited my partner and me to lunch. He didn't like it but said nothing. I think that he had hoped I would have declined the invitation. To his disappointment, I accepted and went with them.

On our way home that evening, my friend and I sat in the back seat of the car as Papa occupied the front seat alone. His jaw was locked. He gave me the cold treatment, which let me know that he was displeased with my behavior. I ignored him and quietly engaged in a conversation with my friend. I knew that sooner or later he would share his thoughts and feelings with me.

Before I completed the thought, the silence was broken. He started to talk about how young men and women were indulging in inappropriate behavior. I tried to ignore him, and to my surprise, I didn't say a word. I allowed him say what he needed to say. But my silence encouraged his tirade. He talked about behaving with honor and dignity as though going to lunch in a mixed group was inappropriate. It seems that the more he talked, the more real his imagination became, and he must have panicked, because to my dismay, he added, "I will not tolerate these things from you. None of my children will come here and disgrace the family or dishonor my name; I'd rather you die instead."

Can you imagine my loving father uttering such cruel words to me? I am not sure what he intended to accomplish by saying them, but I know that I was too hurt and disappointed in him to say a word. My friend looked shocked. She gave me an inquisitive look as to say, "What is this all about?"

Later that evening when we were both calm, Papa came to me and apologized. He explained his concerns, hopes, and dreams for me. He did not want me to do anything that would ruin my chances of attaining my potential. He talked about honor, courage, dignity, and integrity, and reminded me that, "others may but I can't." I forgave him.

❧   ❧   ❧

When it came to Papa's standards, I learned the hard way that it was best to be true to myself. Although Papa and I conceded to each other at times, there were some things he would not compromise on at all. For example, we had to dress "modestly." For Papa, there were certain types of clothes that were not to be worn by his daughters.

Regardless of the activity or temperature outside, hot or cold, we couldn't wear pants. He would remind us that in Deuteronomy 22:5 it says, "A woman must not wear men's clothing, nor a man wear women's clothing, for the Lord your God detests anyone who does this" (NIV).

Papa would say, "Pants are men's clothes, and you are not men." I had to wear a skirt even when I attended sporting events at school. Imagine the looks I received when the kids my age were wearing torn and faded blue jeans. I didn't want to miss the functions, but I was embarrassed when I attended them. It was horrible.

For my high school graduation, someone gave me two pant-suits as gifts. I was elated. I thought that my father would allow me to wear them in order not to offend anyone. The afternoon of my graduation, we were going to the park. I decided to wear one of the pantsuits thinking that it was the most appropriate thing to wear. When we got in the car and my father saw me in pants, he immediately asked me, "What are you wearing?" His look was more like, "Have you lost your mind?" I tried to explain, but he ordered me to "go get dressed."

I responded, "But I am modestly dressed. This is appropriate for the park."

At that moment, everybody in the car turned to look at me. They must have thought I had really lost my mind! I realized that it was futile to plead my case, so I stormed out of the car and went in the house. On the way, I yelled over my shoulder, "I'm not going anymore."

Papa dropped everyone off at the park and came back to the house. He went into his office and called me to join him. I did. I made sure to look very upset. Papa had moved his chair from behind his desk so that he could speak with me. When I entered the room, he was sitting on the chair and calmly said, "Come," with extended arms. When I drew closer, he took my arm, sat me on his lap, and started talking to me. He really tried to convince me to see things his way, but it didn't work. He reminded me that although others were doing it, it didn't mean that I should do it too.

I told him that his rationale didn't make sense to me, and I didn't agree with it. I concluded, "You don't think that women should wear pants, so your daughters especially cannot wear them. I will respect your wishes, and I will not wear pants when I am around you. But I want you to know that the day I leave home, I will wear pants."

He didn't respond. He must have expected to change my mind before I left home. When I was with Papa, I always made sure that

I didn't wear pants. I knew that seeing me in pants would have made him unhappy, so I chose to indulge him. But when I was away, I wore pants with a clear conscience. I never felt dishonest because he knew where I stood. Although I compromised with him, I felt that my integrity was intact.

꿍   꿍   꿍

As far as I can remember, our home was always modestly furnished. Because Papa had learned to make beautiful furniture when he was younger, he played a major role when he and Maman selected furniture for the house. The house was not full of furniture as some of my friends' houses were. When I mentioned to him that we needed more furniture, Papa responded, "I am not committed to furnishing your house. I'm committed to furnishing your mind. What I put in the house will not last and will eventually be taken away. But what I put in your mind, no one can take away. It will last forever."

My father was interested in two things for his children: building our character to honor God and providing us with a good education to serve humankind. Those two things were vital.

Papa strived for excellence and didn't tolerate mediocrity. He wanted us to always do our best in whatever we engaged in. He was tough on us. He told us, "You must always be the head and not the tail." So, whenever we had to perform, we had to give our very best. When it came to our grades, he expected excellence. He would say, "Since God gave you a good functioning brain, you ought to use it to its highest level of potential."

His formula for success was excellence + diligence. He told us repeatedly that if we put effort in everything we did, we could achieve anything. "Hard work and working smart always pay off," he would say. Because I heard it so much, I really believed that I could attain anything in life. Actually, I expected it. Papa wanted us to each choose a profession and reach the highest academic level. He made sacrifices for us to have an education. He met any challenge to help us as long as he saw willingness on our part to achieve. I am not sure how he was able to send all nine of us to private, Christian schools on one salary, but he did it. He wanted the best for us, and he did the impossible to help us reach our goals. He told us that education was our ticket to living the American dream. With education and God on our side, there was no height too great for us to reach. Education was the gateway to greatness, and I believed it.

At the end of my junior year in college, I found out that there were two courses I had to take that summer if I were to graduate the following year. These two courses were not scheduled to be taught again for another two years, so I had to take them right away. I needed seven hundred dollars to enroll, but I didn't have any money. I didn't know what to do, so I called Papa. Without hesitation he said, "Don't worry, you'll have the money."

I went home for the break between the spring and summer sessions. I was home for two weeks. I had a wonderful time with my family, interacting with Papa daily. Never once did he mention anything about the money, and neither did I. The morning of my departure, he called me into his office and handed me seven hundred and fifty dollars. Later, when I found out that he had sold his only car to give me the money, I was shocked.

"Papa, you shouldn't have sold the car. I feel so bad. How are you going to work?" I knew how crucial a car was to a pastor.

He responded, "Ma fille, don't worry, God always provides. You do your part, and I'll do mine."

That summer, I worked hard and gave my best. I wanted my father to know that I appreciated his sacrifice. I appreciated his commitment to my education and treasured his confidence in me. He eventually purchased another car, but I never forgot that experience.

Papa's own educational goals impacted mine. He was in college during most of my high school years. During my first year of college, things became financially challenging in our home to the point where I considered putting college off to get a job. But Papa was determined that I should complete my college education at an Adventist school. Papa decided to put his education on hold, and he went back to work to finance my college education. He eventually completed his program, but he never had the opportunity to achieve his highest educational goal, that of earning a doctoral degree. I determined then that I would complete the highest level of education possible in honor of my father.

Papa was elated when, years later, I told him that I had enrolled in the doctoral program and would be pursuing a doctorate in education. As the years went by, he was my source of inspiration, my support and motivator. And when I procrastinated writing my dissertation, he pushed me forward. I was scheduled to graduate in June 1998, but when I announced to him in April that I was not going to graduate, he became impatient with me.

He said, "You are not taking this seriously. You are wasting time. It is urgent that you get this work completed right away. This is serious." I sensed urgency in his voice. I didn't quite understand why nor did I inquire about it, but I committed to graduating that summer. He prayed with me, and he encouraged and calmed me when I was worried. Against all odds, I completed everything and scheduled an oral defense. On my way to my defense, I called him, and he prayed for me. My father was with me every step of the way.

Papa was present at my graduation. Although he could not see me (he had lost his sight by then), my mother described everything to him. We marched in to "Pomp and Circumstance," wearing our royal blue regalia trimmed in gold and our ornate octagon-shaped cap with its gold tassel. The doctoral candidates carried on their right arm the black velvet hood trimmed in gold. The Commencement ceremony began.

When they called my name and read the title of my dissertation, Papa smiled. I had dedicated my dissertation to him. My advisor hooded me by placing the hood over my head on my shoulder. When she hooded me, she shook my hand and I proceeded to march across the stage and receive my diploma from the president of Andrews University. When the audience broke into applause, Papa was the proudest parent in the room. I was elated, knowing that I had made my father's joy complete. My doctoral degree was for both of us.

Months later I understood why he spoke to me with such urgency in April. His health weakened shortly after returning home to Florida. Two months after my graduation, my father was diagnosed with a brain tumor. He barely recognized me when I rushed to his bedside. I couldn't believe that he could have deteriorated so quickly.

I believe that Papa must have known that his time was near, and he willed himself to be strong so that he could attend my graduation. I would have never imagined that ten months later my father would be buried. He died on June 10, 1999. He would not have participated in one of the most satisfying moments of his parenting experience if I hadn't graduated that summer. I don't think I would have been able to go through graduation without him—I would not have been able to bear the remorse. I am so happy that I made my father proud! Thank God!

❦   ❦   ❦

Although I did not fully embrace Papa's views in my youth, my siblings and I still had to live by the standards he set before us. My siblings and I believed in Papa because he exemplified the standards he set for us. Because of Papa, today I live by my convictions even if I have to stand alone. I now find myself telling my three children the same phrase Papa used to say to me, "Others may, but you cannot." Their reaction is similar to mine when I was younger, but I can't help it. It worked for me, and so far it is working for them as well. They too have learned to honor God and preserve their good names and commit to excellence. I am happy to hear my children acknowledge that they are as thankful that I passed on these values to them as I am to my parents. I hope that they pass it on to their own children: "Others may, but you cannot."

SIX

SAVED FOR A PURPOSE

As a child I used to love story time with Papa. I found the greatest pleasure sitting on his lap, enveloped in his strong arms, as he told my siblings and me his tall tales. These moments were special to me because Papa, being the pastor of many churches, as well as an evangelist, was often away for weeks at a time.

Upon his return from these long trips, we looked forward to hearing all the details. We heard about the people he met, vicariously experiencing the things he did, and we marveled at the miracles that occurred as a result of his prayers and faith. Of course, he always had something for which he could praise God. We would quickly complete our chores and activities in order to spend every possible moment with him. To make his homecoming even more special, my mother cooked extra special dishes, his favorites, of course. After supper and worship, we would all rush to change into our nightclothes and sit with Papa for story time.

My siblings and I would sit around our parents, and each time two of us were selected to sit on their laps. As the family increased to eight children, my mother made sure we all had our turn on their laps. I felt so special when my turn came. I especially looked forward to it because I was afraid of the dark, and sitting on their laps made me feel safe. After everyone was comfortably seated, we waited with baited breath for Papa to begin his story.

We sat together, enveloped by the darkness, listening intently, laughing uproariously, and singing heartily. As I reminisce on these particular vignettes of my life, I am filled with nostalgia. If I close my eyes, I can still see the shape of the moon and the stars twinkling in the darkened sky. The scene was absolutely breathtaking. The sweet melody of the birds and insects echoing from the garden and surrounding woods reminded me of a woodwind ensemble. I especially loved the explosion of lights generated by the fireflies. All these natural activities, including the nagging mosquitoes, added to the spellbinding effect Papa's wonderful stories had on us. In those moments my father was like Superman to me, coming home from his escapades of rescuing the world. He was my hero.

Papa loved to quote poetry and passages as he shared stories and tales. Some stories were of a biographical nature while others were biblical, historical, folkloric, or humorous. He was a masterful raconteur. Through those stories, Papa grounded us in our heavenly and earthly heritage, evoked patriotism and pride in our history, and inspired courage, love, devotion, and service to God and humanity. He sang songs, and we cheerfully chimed along. He added humor, and we cried as we laughed intensely. He twisted our mind with riddles and puzzles, patiently waiting for us to uncover them. He didn't waste a moment, making good use of time. There were times when Papa allowed us to select our favorite stories, which we repeatedly requested. My favorite was about a defining moment in my parents' history.

One of the ways through which I communicate is storytelling. I discovered that this love of telling stories came from my early childhood experience of listening to my father's stories. Even in telling us stories, he utilized techniques to stretch our minds and teach us lessons in unforgettable ways. When my children were younger, I engaged in the same practice with them, and they loved it as well. Storytelling is also interwoven in my public speaking presentations, as I found this technique to be an effective way of getting my point across. I have now become skillful at it. I thank my father for developing my passion for storytelling.

৵৽   ৵৽   ৵৽

As exciting as those evenings were, I was always the first to retire. My younger siblings were wide awake, but I needed my sleep. As a result I would always fall asleep whenever I sat on either of my parents' laps. When I would sit with my siblings, I would retire early to sleep on my parents' bed while the rest of the family remained on the porch. I would dive under the sheets and fall asleep. At the end of the story time, Papa would come into the room and carry me to my bed.

One night while I was fast asleep on my parents' bed, my 4-year-old brother Naasson came into the room and noticed a matchbox on the nightstand. Even though he had been warned many times by Maman to stay away from them, Naasson was fascinated with matches. He must have been going through a curiosity stage, as all children do. In spite of the many warnings, he still decided to inspect the matchbox more closely. Naasson must have forgotten that I was sleeping in the middle of the bed. He sat on the edge of the bed staring at the box for a while; then, the inevitable happened. Naasson succumbed to temptation and struck one match after another until one finally lit. He held the lit match until the heat got too close to his fingers. He then dropped it on the bed, which instantly caught on fire. The entire bed became engulfed by the blaze.

Meanwhile, my family was enjoying more of Papa's tales on the back porch. All of a sudden, Maman said, "I smell smoke."

Then, turning to the others, she asked, "Do you smell it? It's coming from the house!"

Thank God for mother's super-sensitive nose! Everyone ran into the house and discovered that the smell was coming from the master bedroom. As they reached the door, they saw the flames.

At the sight of the bed, Maman screamed, "Jesus, my child is dead!" They sent for firemen, but Papa refused to wait. He tried to put the fire out by himself with sheets and blankets. He succeeded. Papa put me on the floor to examine me. In the midst of this ruckus, I woke up. To his amazement, not a hair on my body was singed. I was not injured. Yet, the mattress on which I laid and the sheets that wrapped me were burnt. Everyone was dumbfounded. By that time the firemen had arrived, they couldn't believe their eyes. God performed a miracle and saved my life!

Papa tried to calm everyone down, so he gathered us together to thank God for saving my life. Before prayer Papa drew me close to him and said to me, "God saved you from death today. He wanted you to experience that He will always be with you. Even when you walk through the valley of the shadow of death, He will be with you. Most importantly, God has a purpose for your life. He has something great for you to do. Always remember that God saved you from that fire for a purpose"

After that eventful incident, my family and I continued to enjoy our wonderful evenings on the porch. However, I cannot recall ever leaving the porch alone again. I made sure that someone was with me when I went to my parents' bed; otherwise, I fell asleep on the chair and retired at the same time as everyone else.

It was customary for my family to gather together for a praise and thanksgiving service whenever God blessed us in a particular way. Papa always presented a lesson for us to learn from each grand experience. At my father's death, he passed on the mantel to my mother, and to this day my family operates that way. Similarly,

I follow this practice in my home. I have taught my children to think of God first in all experiences of their lives and praise Him continuously for coming to their rescue in times of need. I believe that's what my father intended for his children to learn. He wanted this practice to become a natural expression of who we are, and he succeeded.

SEVEN

LIVING A LIFE OF PURPOSE

L iving a life based on God-given purpose was the theme of Papa's life. This theme translated into loving God supremely, serving Him, and of course, serving mankind. He was consumed by that purpose, that one singular focus. God was the central figure in everything he did. His every thought, action, and deed was seen through Jesus Christ. He strove to be like God. He truly was an unusual man.

Likewise, he wanted his children to live a life of purpose ordained by God. Very early in life, he wanted us to be aware of our purpose, and he did his best to steer us in that direction. He taught us to have a relationship with God, to live our lives through Christ, and to serve God by serving humanity. Papa always reminded me that God saved me from the fire because He had a purpose for my life.

Whenever I misbehaved or was headed in a direction that was contrary to God's will for me, he cautioned me, "God's daughter cannot behave this way. Everything you do has to be done for His honor and glory. Don't displease Him. You are being prepared for ministry. You need to remember that before you act." Although my brothers and sisters didn't share my experience of almost being burned to death, they were also told these same inspiring words, "God has a purpose for your life."

For a long time I wondered what God's purpose was for me. I grew up to believe Papa's words. I somehow expected that when God revealed my purpose to me He would engage me in a life mission that was extraordinary. I thought, "Why else would He have saved my life?" As I grew older, and life's challenges began to weigh me down, Papa comforted me with these words, "God is preparing you for service." At times I became frustrated and wished that Papa would have temporary amnesia so he wouldn't remind me of God's purpose one more time. I was often haunted by Papa's words. He intentionally programmed me to live a purpose-focused life.

As the years went by I developed a burning desire to know what God's plan was for my life. I asked God on numerous occasions to reveal His plan for my life, but I didn't receive any clear directions. For a while I thought that God's purpose for my life would have been manifested through my career. Therefore, I had to choose it carefully. My decisions had to be based on God's will for me. When I reached high school, I decided that I would pursue a career in medicine.

At the beginning of my senior year, a medical missionary visited our church and shared his experiences with us. He recounted numerous miracles that God had performed through him and his fellow missionaries: people were healed, sometimes miraculously, and many accepted Jesus Christ as their personal savior and were baptized. He emphasized how great the need was for medical doctors in the mission fields. Finally, he made an appeal, asking people to choose the mission field. He pleaded, "There are so many, many needs. Allow God to work through you." He then said the magic words, "He will do great things through you."

Along with Papa's deep bass voice, the missionary's words echoed in my mind, day and night. I felt impressed to go into medicine and become a medical missionary in Africa. I thought, *This must be the sign. God must be speaking to me. It must be His purpose for my life. Surely God will use me there.*

Then, during my last semester in high school, I enrolled in a health course that was required for graduation. One day my health teacher showed the class a film about the effects of smoking on the lungs. The film was an actual surgical procedure on a man with lung cancer, which was caused by excessive smoking. I became increasingly nauseous as I watched the gory details of that surgery. I almost fainted at the sight of his black lungs covered with so much blood. When I couldn't stomach it any longer, I rushed out of the classroom.

After class, my well-meaning teacher approached me, and with concern in his voice, he said, "Are you sure you want to be a doctor?" When I responded positively, he berated me with more tough questions to which I had no answers. "You want to be a doctor and you can't even watch a simple surgery? What will you do when you go to medical school? How are you going to handle real life situations? I recommend that you consider another career. Medicine is not for you."

I was convinced that God was speaking to me through my teacher. Furthermore, I thought, *Why else would I be so fearful of blood? If He wanted me to become a doctor, He would remove that fear.*

My dream to be a medical missionary died with my teacher's admonition. If medicine was not the answer, then what was it? It was frustrating not to have a clear direction from God at this stage of my educational life. I was a senior on my way to college, and I had no major in mind. What was God's purpose for me? What did He want from me? Time was running out. So I consulted with

Papa concerning my frustration. He responded softly, "'For I know the plans I have for you,' declares the Lord, 'plans to prosper you and not to harm you, plans to give you hope and a future' (Jeremiah 29:11, NIV). Be calm, ma fille, and listen for His directions. He will tell you. Just be patient. He will guide you. By the way, God's purpose for you is not only about your career."

"What do you mean?" I was confounded.

"Serving others through your career is only one aspect of God's purpose for you. It is about who you are and what you do under *all* circumstances. It involves all aspects of your whole self. That's what I have been teaching you all along." I didn't understand, but Papa assured me that in time I would.

Papa had a way of making such statements and leaving us puzzled to figure it out for ourselves. He claimed that it would be more meaningful if we uncovered it on our own. Well, I sat there looking frustrated. He felt sorry for me and said, "Now, let's explore your career options." Papa began to ask me questions like, "What do you love to do the most? What are you passionate about? What are some of the things you are interested in?"

We discussed some of my interests and goals. We examined my personality and temperament. Papa asked more questions to help me clarify my thoughts. He indicated that I should follow the career that called me. Then he got up from the couch and left the room saying, "You are doing well, ma fille. Continue to dwell in the inquiry with God, and He will guide your steps."

I was very impatient. I wondered what and how God was going to communicate with me. Would God speak to me audibly? Would He send a messenger to relate a message to me? Would He communicate to me through dreams? Graduation was in a few months, and I hadn't chosen a major. I was told that if I wanted to be successful in college, I needed to choose a profession before entering college. I wanted somebody to tell me what to do. Papa, who loved to tell me what to do, didn't indulge me this time.

I continued to investigate other professions. I began to seriously consider law. When my siblings got into trouble with my parents, I jumped to their defense. At times Papa and Maman would ask me, "Are you the lawyer of this family? What makes you think that you have to come to everybody's defense?" Moreover, after examining myself, I realized that I enjoyed conversing, debating, and winning; I thrived best when I was around people; and I wanted to make a difference in people's lives. Law seemed like the perfect career for me.

However, I didn't think that Papa would approve of that choice. I believed that he would have challenged me on it, insisting that law was definitely not God's will for me. With enough persistence, I would have deferred to him. Although I could have been an exceptional lawyer, I let go of the idea. In retrospect, I realize that I didn't even broach the subject with Papa. I made a prejudgment about him and believed it to be true. Years later, when I shared this with Papa, he responded, "You could have been an extraordinary lawyer." How unfortunate.

Papa strongly supported my sister Jasmine in her choice to go to law school, and today she is an attorney. Ironically, I am frequently told, "You missed your calling. You should have been a lawyer." Periodically, I have this strong urge to apply to law school, but I banish the thought instantly. At this point in my life, I am fulfilled in my profession.

One day it occurred to me that I had not investigated teaching. Teaching was a noble profession. I considered its advantages and disadvantages. The biggest advantage, having the summer to spend time with my children, was very appealing to me. Additionally, I loved to talk and impart "wisdom" to others. Teaching fit my personality and temperament. *Children need to be around positive and happy people so they can emulate these characteristics,* I thought. *I could make learning fun for them. I could enjoy teaching for a long time.*

I thought of Mrs. Phillips, my tenth grade English teacher. One afternoon she assigned us to write a poem by the end of the period. Since it was my second year in the U.S., I was not proficient in English. I usually carried my French/English dictionary with me, but unfortunately, I had forgotten it that day. I just couldn't think of the English words fast enough to complete the assignment on time. I felt like I couldn't think in English at all! I tried, but I couldn't compose one complete sentence. I froze.

As the clock ticked away, I became increasingly frustrated and began to sob. I didn't want my classmates to notice me crying, because some of them would have welcomed the opportunity to ridicule me. They would sing out, "Polly wants a cracker, Polly wants a cracker." So I sobbed quietly, shielding my tears from their view.

However, Mrs. Phillips noticed me. She approached my desk, leaned toward me, and whispered, "Having some problems with the assignment?"

"Yes," I muttered, "I forgot my dictionary at home, and I can't think of the right words in English."

With a reassuring voice, she proposed, "How about you finish it at home and bring it tomorrow."

I felt better. As a result, the whole class got the same extension, and everyone was happy. I went home and effortlessly wrote the poem in French, and then I translated it into English. This process required more time to complete my work, but I had better control over the product.

The following day, I was anxious to turn in my assignment. Mrs. Phillips winked at me as she collected my poem. The next day she returned the corrected assignments to my classmates one by one. My heart was palpitating with anticipation. All the students received their poems. She went back to her desk without giving me mine. I thought, *Oh no, the poem was terrible!* I was crushed, but no one seemed to notice. I said nothing, fearing the jokes from the other students. I would have died of embarrassment. So I decided to wait until everyone else left after class to inform Mrs. Phillips that I hadn't received my poem.

However, as Mrs. Phillips reached her desk, she exclaimed, "Class, I am very pleased with the poems you wrote yesterday. I decided to read one of them for you because I found it to be exceptional." She began to read my poem with expression, and it sounded pretty good! My heart leaped with joy, and I couldn't stop smiling while the tears rolled down my cheeks. I was touched by her sensitive, reassuring gesture. When she finished reading my poem, she walked to my desk, handed it to me, and said, "Great job, Pollyanna!"

My eyes filled with tears, my nose running, I sputtered, "Thank-thank you."

The class exploded with applause, and Mrs. Phillips returned to her desk to begin the day's lesson.

I was so grateful for that experience. After leaving Haiti I spent two years learning a strange language and adjusting to a different culture. I thought of myself as inadequate and even stupid. I questioned my ability to perform well academically. By this experience, I had no self-esteem left. In two years I had moved from gifted to learning disabled. I was no longer the proud, talented, and popular student that I used to be. I only had two friends: one spoke my native languages while the other one I could hardly communicate with; she was American. I understood English fairly well, but I just couldn't express myself well enough. I was starting all over again. That was mental and emotional torture. That was a difficult thing for a sixteen-year-old girl to do. It was excruciatingly frustrating!

Mrs. Phillips restored my faith in myself. My dormant self-esteem resurfaced. I became popular at least in my English class. I worked harder than ever, learned English proficiently, and regained my confidence. That happened because of a teacher. On the annals of my history, Mrs. Phillips remained one of my favorite teachers. She made a remarkable difference in my life, and I cherished her and the poem that started it all for a long time. I resolved that if I could touch students' lives as profoundly as Mrs. Phillips touched mine, I would love to be a teacher. God would surely approve of teaching as a way to make a difference for Him. In that moment, questions concerning my career vanished. It was as if all the pieces of the puzzle finally fit together. I was certain that God led me to this decision, and I was at peace.

So I went to college to become a teacher. Interestingly, Papa approved, never questioning my choice. When I announced it to him, he smiled and said nothing. That was his sign of approval. He encouraged and supported me along the years.

Later, when I became a teacher, I began to question if teaching was really my life's calling. I didn't think that this "great thing" for which God saved my life could take place in a classroom. I had no idea where, but it had to occur someplace else. I waited a while for God's revelation to me. Meanwhile I continued to teach. Little did I realize that great things—miracles—were happening in my classroom.

Take for example, Jamaal, a sixth grader who could not read when he entered my classroom one September. He was shy, didn't want to participate in reading activities, and hated school. I stayed after school to give him extra help. He said to me, "I am a dummy. Why are you wasting your time with me? Nobody else did before."

I had compassion for this boy. He really wanted to learn to read, but he believed that he couldn't because of the way others had caused him to think of himself. I wondered, *What happened to this child before he came to my class? How could his teachers allow him to move from one grade to another when he was illiterate?*

This was his first year in our school. His mother, realizing that Jamaal's needs were not being met at the local public school, decided to send him to a Seventh-day Adventist school. I encouraged him, prayed with him, and called him a genius. Jamaal's attitude changed as his reading improved. It was fascinating to watch his transformation.

About mid-year, his mother came to visit me. She said, "I never thought I'd see the day when Jamaal would look forward to going to school. He talks about you all the time and can't wait to come to your class. The boy is so confident in himself; he reads to me every day! He never wanted to do that before. Thank you! Thank you for what you're doing for my child! Nobody seemed to care. I was afraid that I would lose this child! But you care. I'm so glad I brought him to this school! God bless you!"

By the end of the school year, Jamaal was participating in reading activities in the classroom. Although he had not reached his grade level, he was not embarrassed to read in front of his classmates. He was confident and very cooperative in the classroom. When Jamaal moved to the seventh grade, I continued to tutor him for free until he was reading at the appropriate grade level. He became a bright and confident young man. I was to him what Mrs. Phillips was to me.

This is only one example of the numerous transformations that occurred in my classrooms. I was satisfied and felt that impacting a child's life to such an extent was a worthwhile career. I felt that God had called me to be in the classroom, and I never regretted choosing education. Thirty years later, I am still an educator. Education is indeed a noble profession. As a teacher, I partner with God in shaping and molding diverse young minds into His likeness. I create a landscape that opens up endless possibilities for my students. I am at awe at the results that God has produced through me at the end of each school year.

However, I was not fully satisfied that education was my only life's purpose. Based on my father, it had to be more than a career. I was still searching for the answer to the big question of my life: What was God's purpose for my life?

ॐ   ॐ   ॐ

I kept looking for God's purpose. Could it be parenting? Mothering is the noblest of all roles. It seemed to me that shaping a child's character, fashioning him into a respectable God-fearing and productive human being was an extraordinary thing for any person to do. My gynecologist said that I would not be able to have children. However, I got pregnant within the first month that I was married. My husband and I decided that I would put my career on hold for a while to become a full-time mom. I thought that Byron, my firstborn child, was a miracle, so I didn't expect to have another child. Five months after his birth, I became pregnant again. After David's birth, I realized that I had no problems getting pregnant and I needed to use contraceptives.

When David turned one, we decided to have our last child. I wanted a daughter more than anything, so I prayed for one. Shortly after my prayer, I became pregnant. I was convinced that God had answered my prayer. Of course, He did. My beautiful Gabrielle was born, and for three days I had three children under three years of age.

Being a parent, a mother, was an awesome responsibility. I was always mindful of the fact that my children were fashioning themselves after me. I had to be careful of every word uttered and every deed performed. For a while I thought that mothering, training, and educating three well-rounded, God-fearing children was the answer to my question about God's purpose for my life. Therefore, I took my role of mothering seriously. God had blessed me with three beautiful, healthy jewels to train, and I wasn't about to leave their upbringing to chance or to other people.

Mothering three babies was a joy and a challenge. I fully committed myself to the task. Good and effective parenting doesn't occur through metamorphosis. You don't wake up one morning and become a good parent. It takes intentional effort and hard work. I was determined to learn as much as I could to do the job. I only had one opportunity to parent these three children. My upbringing was always my first resource. I compared my parenting style and practices to that of my parents. I continuously drew gems from their example. When I was accused of being too tough, I remembered accusing my parents. When I was blamed for sheltering them too much, I remembered my parents' practices. When I was told by friends that I needed to expose my children to a variety of literature other than the Bible, I remembered Maman sending me to a corner to memorize a complete psalm as a timeout. I figured that my parents must have done a good job since I turned out well. Repeating those practices with my children would not hurt them.

I read numerous books on parenting and prayed without ceasing. I am so grateful that I had a community that supported me in raising my children. Whenever I needed help, I talked to Maman, Maman-in-law, and my contemporaries, and of course, I read more books. When I needed a break or a babysitter, one my sisters were always available.

When my children reached school age, I homeschooled them. I thought, *Who better to teach my children than me? After all, I am a teacher.* They finally attended conventional schools when they reached eighth, sixth, and fifth grades, respectively.

When they went to school, I didn't consider my parenting job to be complete. I became more diligent in parenting because now my children were exposed to other influences. Although I sent them to church school, it was my responsibility to be their parent. I was involved in every aspect of their experiences. Although I was a full-time doctoral student, they were my priority.

My husband and I have been an integral part of our children's lives every step of the way. Today, I can testify that God has blessed us with three wonderful young-adult children. They are not perfect, far from it, but God is gracious. I can truly say that it was worth the trip! Now, that we no longer play the parenting role in our children's lives, Baldwin and I enjoy playing the roles of counselor, consultant, and friend. When they call—which they regularly do for various reasons—we are available to support them as they build their own lives.

I really believe that God called me to be a mom. It's been and continues to be one of the most gratifying and challenging experiences of my life. Parenting has given me a glimpse of God's love and increased my understanding of and appreciation for God and my own parents. I am convinced that I served God by raising three of His future disciples. I shaped lives that would impact the world someday. For me, mothering was, and still is, a divine calling.

Papa was very proud of me as a parent. He was amused at the way I interacted with my children. One day he said to me, "You are so patient with the children. It pleases me to see how you spend so much time teaching them of God. What a good mother you've become! I never thought you had it in you."

I took it as a compliment. It was his way of giving me positive feedback and telling me that he was proud of me. Coming from Papa it meant the world to me.

ख़ॖ   ख़ॖ   ख़ॖ

There was a time when I underwent a serious challenge in my life. Papa was visiting, so we spent considerable time together. I confided in him about my experience, and during one of our lengthy tête-à-tête (heart-to-heart conversations), he said, "You will get through this, ma fille. The pain will not last forever. Go through it with grace, and remember, nothing happens to us by chance. God is preparing you for ministry. There is a lesson to be learned from this experience. Every experience prepares you to be a better servant and make your ministry more meaningful."

Spoken at that moment, those words made no difference to me. I thought that he was going to remind me of God's purpose for my life, and I was ready to tell him "enough already." But, when I recovered, I was able to support those who were experiencing the same type of pain and disappointment. It's as though I was attracting people who had similar experiences. Many people shared their struggles with me, and I did likewise.

As I was "ministering" to other people's needs, I remembered Papa's words and understood. God was preparing me to serve on another level, a deeper level. I became more compassionate, accepting, and forgiving. I fully surrendered to God's will and told Him that I was ready. Then I waited for the time when God was finally going to cash in on His investment. It never came as I had expected. As I grew closer to God, I began to realize that God's purpose for me was not to do some grandiose and extraordinary thing. God wanted me to be faithful to Him in every aspect of my life at every moment, and as I learned from life's experiences, I used my talents to the best of my ability to serve others.

I began to reflect on my life, and I realized that I had been living God's purpose all along. He used me in many situations: as a daughter, sister, wife, mother, friend, educator, administrator, public speaker, and Christian woman. I wondered how I could have missed it all those years. So that's what Papa was referring to! It was so simple!

I also realized that God expected the same from all His children, not just me. He saved my life as He saves many lives on a daily basis. I was no different than anyone else. This revelation offered me a different perspective from which to live life. I finally got the answer to my life's question. When I shared this revelation with Papa, he responded, "Bravo, ma fille! It is good for you to discover God for yourself. When God reveals truths to you directly, you will be convicted. I have been observing you every step of the way. You have become a mature Christian. You have been living God's purpose, and He has been doing great things through you. Benit soit L'Eternel!" (May the Lord be praised!)

Papa helped me to live a God-consumed life. He was instrumental in the path that my life followed. Both Papa and Maman used my experiences to point out God and life's lessons to me. Because of their instruction, I learned to listen for God's voice and guidance. As a result, I became a better Christian, and I now serve Him fully.

EIGHT

GIFTED TONGUE

In the history of gifted orators, names such as Dr. Martin Luther King Jr., Billy Graham, Winston Churchill, Mahatma Gandhi, Nelson Mandela, and Barack Obama are inscribed with reverence. They set the standards which others follow and are compared to. I have come to the realization that what made them so impactful was not only the content of their speeches or the delivery but that they were being true to their calling. They were focused. My father was like them in that way, and I can undoubtedly include him on the list of great speakers.

As long as I can remember, Papa was a preacher. He loved to preach. He was passionate about preaching. He knew that he was called to be a preacher, and whenever he stood behind the pulpit to preach, he was in his element.

Preaching was Papa's passion. At numerous occasions he declared, "The day I stop preaching the gospel is the day I will die." He loved to preach so much that I imagined him dying behind the pulpit after offering his last sermon. I figured that it would be the best way for him to go, doing the thing he loved the most. When I mentioned that to him, he just smiled. He stopped preaching when his brain could no longer function properly. Then he died.

Wherever Papa preached, the church was filled beyond capacity. It was partly because people flocked around to hear him preach. Wherever he was invited to speak, people came from everywhere to hear. His reputation preceded him in French and Haitian communities: he was the premier Haitian evangelist in Haiti, Quebec, Canada, and the U.S. He transcended race, culture, and gender barriers; his messages were powerful and effective wherever he went. Thousands of souls were baptized as a result of his evangelistic efforts. He entered territories where there were no Seventh-day Adventist churches and planted several fellowships of believers before being reassigned. When he was assigned to a small church, the membership immediately multiplied. I am convinced that he was called and chosen by God to be a preacher of the gospel.

When we lived in Nebraska, Papa was not as fluent in English as he was in French, not even close. However, he didn't allow his lack of mastery of the language to deter him from preaching the gospel. While preaching, if he got stuck on a word he didn't know in English, the audience would shout words to him until he identified the appropriate one. At first, I used to be embarrassed by these scenes. But to him, it didn't matter. He was more committed to his calling than to what others would think of him. As long as people were blessed, and indeed they were, he was not deterred by the challenges of speaking a new language.

While he preached, I watched the congregation, and they didn't seem to mind the fact that he struggled with the language. In fact, they were grateful for having contributed to a masterpiece. Sometimes I thought the pastors wouldn't invite him back to preach because of the language barrier, but they did over and over. He was so loved that he was a member of two churches. They both wanted him to be at their church, but they decided that they would rather share him than not have him at all. God still spoke through him powerfully, even in a strange language. The Holy Spirit is no respecter of language, creed, or race. He will work wonders through anyone who is willing.

Papa had a way of captivating the audience from the first word he uttered to his last. Sometimes, when he told Bible stories, it felt like I had never heard them before. His audiences echoed the same sentiments. One day he was preaching about love and forgiveness, and he told the story of the encounter between Jacob and Esau after their years of separation. Adults and children alike were seating on the edge of their seats; even I was in awe. He captured the attention of his entire audience, young and old, man and woman. He told the story with such expression and passion that each person became a living spectator of the event, sitting in the presence of Jacob and Esau. The eloquence and passion with which the story was told, the poignancy of the message, the clarification of background information and historical events, the distinction of particular elements usually left unnoticed, altogether created synergy in the room. The energy in the room was palpable. I never heard it told in that manner. It was extraordinary.

Papa took the most obscure biblical passage and made it so simple that even the dumb would understand. Papa's purpose in preaching was to bring people to a better understanding of God, which would lead them to surrender their lives to His will. When Papa completed his sermons, his intent was invariably accomplished. Papa was a preacher par excellence.

One of the remarkable qualities that Papa acquired was his knowledge of the Bible. He committed his Bible to memory. He was like the encyclopedia of the Bible. If you named a topic, he would find the text.

There were times he tried to visit a church incognito, but once someone in the room recognized him, they would notify the pastor of the church who would publicly invite him to preach. The people would applaud to influence his response. Of course, he never declined. What fascinated me most was the fact that my father could preach exceptionally well without notes and at the spur of the moment. It was as though he had prepared for weeks. I was always amazed when he did that. When I would approach him afterwards, I would say, "Papa, did you know that you were going to preach?"

"No"

"So you didn't write a sermon or at least have sermon notes. How did you do that? How can you preach so well without a written sermon? You are such a great preacher!"

"Non, ma fille. God did it. That's what happens when you submit yourself to the workings of the Holy Spirit."

Any success he achieved was credited to God.

༺ɔ   ༺ɔ   ༺ɔ

Papa lost his sight three years prior to his death, but even after that, he preached and conducted evangelistic series, weekly revivals, and weeks of prayer. When he officially retired in 1997 and moved to Florida, we thought that he had finally stopped preaching. But it only seemed to get worse. He was on high demand, preaching in numerous churches and holding revivals for months in a row. Churches were packed. We, as a family, didn't appreciate that. We had hoped that finally he would give us all his time and attention. However, since we knew that preaching made him happy, we deferred.

Since Papa couldn't see, he preached without his Bible, sermon notes, or any kind of aid. He regurgitated Bible texts and passages and preached without hesitation. The quality and power of his sermons did not diminish. In fact, people marveled even more at his knowledge of the Bible, and they were inspired to study it as well. He told them to "develop the gifts that God gives you while you can so that you can still use them if you lose your vital senses." The audience would applaud, and he'd continue with his sermon.

In the end, Papa succumbed to a brain tumor, which slowly took over his mind. During the last months of his life, he lost his memory and didn't recognize anyone, not even my mother. His mind seemed to regress to childhood. Yet, he remembered his Bible. When my sisters and I visited him, we would read Bible passages to him, and he would recite them as we read along. I stopped at various intervals to test him. He would continue his recital until the passage ended; then he would stop without uttering a word. I just couldn't comprehend how his decaying mind couldn't recognize the voice of his children, of his wife of 49 years, or of his only brother, yet he could remember Bible passages word for word. Unbelievable!

When I heard Papa speak, I used to say to myself, "Someday I want to preach like that." Such an occasion occurred one Sabbath morning when my husband was scheduled to preach. Although he had the flu, he insisted that it was his responsibility to deliver the word of God on that day. In spite of my advice to stay home, he said that he would be alright.

When the time came for the divine service to begin, the elders marched in without Baldwin. When I didn't see him after half an hour, I became concerned and inquired from an officiating deacon as to Baldwin's whereabouts. He told me that he was not doing well and was resting until it was time for him to preach. I immediately went to his office and found him in worse condition than he was before. He was coughing incessantly.

I asked him to have one of the elders preach, and he told me that he had tried. They said that they couldn't preach because they were not prepared. I couldn't believe that none of them would try. When I realized that Baldwin couldn't preach, I told him that I would take his place. When he did not protest, I knew for sure that he was really sick.

I chose a text and prayed that God would speak through me. When the time came for the sermon, I stepped behind the pulpit and preached a full sermon. I know that God worked through me based on the responses I received from people. After the service, the first elder told me, "I cannot believe that you preached so powerfully without any notes or preparation. I refused to preach because of that, but you didn't let that stop you. You inspire me. I am going to prepare myself so that I can be like you. Thank you." My wish to speak extemporaneously like Papa came true.

Now that I have become a public speaker, I often tell myself, as I stand in front of an audience, "I was born for this." Sometimes when I speak, I catch Papa in me. Obviously, in watching him preach all those years, I consciously and unconsciously learned from him. I can't help but emulate him.

While he was alive, every time I preached or spoke, he was eager to hear about it. He would ask me all types of questions about my presentation. Sometimes I would go to him for information and advice while preparing for a speech or sermon. He felt honored that I still valued "the mind of an old man," as he put it.

He would always ask about the audience response. That part meant a lot to him. Then he would say, "Praise the Lord! Bravo, my daughter. God worked through you once more. I am proud of you."

His response affirmed me. I wanted so much for him to approve of my sermons. He knew that I was gifted, and he never uttered a disparaging word. He always encouraged me to pursue what I felt called to do or be. I have not reached Papa's level of mastery and delivery in speaking, but I get a sense of how he felt when he was in the zone: the feeling of coming alive with each word. It's an awesome experience to be so connected to God that you let yourself go and let God speak through you!

The last words I spoke to Papa were as follows: "Papa, Baldwin and I will continue the work that you started. Don't worry; your work has not ended. It has just begun."

My father mustered all the strength he had to respond, "Uh huh." His response was loud and clear and filled with emotion. I knew that he heard me and approved. Now, as I travel all over the world preaching, I speak for God and in honor of Papa, who was my inspiration.

When Papa died on that Thursday in June, I had a previous speaking engagement in Toronto, Canada, for the weekend starting that Friday. Although I knew that his illness was terminal, the reality of his death was devastating. Later on during the day, I remembered that I had to catch a flight the next morning. I had to decide whether I would go or cancel my engagement.

I rationalized, "They would understand if I didn't make the appointment. After all, I just lost my father. No one would be so cruel as to expect so much from another human being. They will understand. In fact, they will empathize with me. It will be OK if I don't go."

Then I had to grapple with the fact that it was too close to the event for me to back down. They were celebrating women, and I was the guest speaker for the whole weekend. It might be difficult for them to locate another female speaker in such short notice. But what could I do?

The only reasonable thing to do was for me to graciously give my regrets to the church. Then I wondered, "What would people say if I showed up in the face of my father's death? Would they think of me as heartless? Would they say that I didn't love my father?" That very thought stopped me in my tracks for a moment.

Then I thought, "What better way is there to honor my father's life than to preach after his death? Didn't I tell him a few days before that I would carry on the work that he began?" So, I decided to honor my papa by preaching.

On Sabbath morning during the divine worship hour, I shared with the audience about my relationship with my dad and told them of his recent death. I believe the fact that I kept my promise in the face of my situation caused the audience to listen to me in a more powerful way.

I didn't break down during the three speeches I presented. I was in a zone, especially on Saturday morning. It felt as though I was outside of myself observing the whole scene. I was aware of my feelings, my thoughts, and my actions. When I felt overwhelmed by my sadness, I was able to stay under control by reminding myself of my purpose for being there. I was also conscious of the impact that I had on my listeners. How I left them was important to me as well. I guess it can be said that I was undauntedly courageous.

At the end of the weekend, I was filled with satisfaction and fulfillment. I knew that I had represented Papa well. I knew that if Papa were alive he would have been proud of me. I was proud to honor my father. And though he wasn't there to tell me audibly, in my heart I heard him say to me, "Tu es une femme de substance. Tu peux tout realiser dans la vie. Comme Je suis fier de toi!" (You are a woman of substance. You will achieve anything you desire in life. How proud I am of you!) That was good enough for me.

My father lived a life completely submitted to the Holy Spirit, and he spoke powerfully based on that relationship. He and God had a connection that was rare. This connection was so evident in his sermons. The Bible was his textbook, and he memorized it to ensure that God's words were heard when he spoke. He would study the Word, make in-depth preparation, and leave the delivery to God. That was my father's life, and it is now my own.

NINE

MY HOME THE INN

Hospitality was demonstrated in our home—visitors and the needy could move in at any moment's notice. Papa believed that our house was an inn free of charge. We always lived in spacious houses because we were a large family. Moreover, Papa must have bought these large houses so that there would always be enough room for people to stay in as long as they needed. As far back as I can remember, we cared for and entertained numerous guests and relatives in our house.

Some guests stayed for the duration of a weekend up to a few months. Some were in need of a place to live in order to go to school or to work and build up some funds to recover from financial challenges. Others visited while they were vacationing. Their vacation was an opportune time to retreat for a week of prayer with Papa and Maman. Fewer people came when we were in the U.S., but we had our share of guests in Haiti and Canada. That's how my parents taught me about hospitality. Papa's motto was, "It is more blessed to give than to receive."

I remember one instance in Haiti when Mr. Louis and his family moved in to our home. They were experiencing financial challenges, and he must have shared his plight with Papa. For days the servants prepared the third floor of the house, which, at the time, was not in use. Finally, we watched a family move in. A whole family of six descended on us.

We, the children, didn't like having people up there because we felt that they were invading our privacy. Papa and Maman told us to play with the children even though we didn't want to. They wanted us to be hospitable. They wanted to make sure that the people didn't feel unwelcome or uncomfortable. Mr. Louis and his family lived with us for six months. Truthfully, the house was big enough for them to live without any invasion of our privacy. We lived separate lives in separate quarters, but we ate our meals together every day.

Another time, when we were living in Montreal, Papa received a telephone call around 11:00 p.m. and went out shortly after the call. Maman immediately came upstairs to Jean's room and began to fix the bed. Jean was attending school at Kingsway College in Ontario. Maman informed us that Josette, a young pregnant woman who was a member of Papa's church, was in need of a place to live. Her husband left her penniless. Since she wasn't working, she was evicted from her apartment. She had no one and nowhere to go. Of course, Papa and Maman rescued her.

Josette came in that night and lived with us for more than a year until she was able to find a job and save enough money to get an apartment. As a result, my sisters, Jasmine and Evangeline, were misplaced. The basement had a bedroom, but my father felt that it was not appropriate for our guests to stay there while we were comfortable upstairs. There were seven bedrooms in the house, and all of them were occupied. The basement was unoccupied, but it was not good enough for the guests. Because she was pregnant, Maman took good care of her. She and anyone who stayed in our home never paid for their keep. We made her feel at home and enjoyed watching the metamorphosis of a slender woman turn into a full-blown pregnant one.

On another occasion my sister Evangeline brought a friend home. At the time, my sister was a student at Kingsway College and was working as a colporteur in Quebec City to raise funds for school. During this time, she met Stephanie who became her close friend. Stephanie was in a situation where she couldn't return to her previous dwelling place. She was living with a family where she cared for their children. She wanted to get an education, but her employer wouldn't allow her to. Since she was working towards residency, she had no recourse, until she heard of a summer program where students could sell books and use the money toward their education. She seized the opportunity and left to join the program.

Unfortunately, at the end of the summer, Stephanie had neither a school to attend nor enough money to take care of herself. She refused to return to take care of children without the hope of acquiring an education. At 18 years of age, she was homeless. Evangeline called home to share her new friend's plight with Papa and requested to bring her home to live with us. Papa briefly consulted Maman and responded cheerfully, "Bring her; bring her with you."

At the end of the summer, Evangeline arrived at home and brought a new addition to the family with her. Papa was ecstatic that his children were getting infected by his spirit of compassion and hospitality. He expressed his contentment and uttered his favorite praise, "Benit soit L'Eternel!"

Stephanie moved in and intentionally worked hard to become integrated in the family. She was special. She was the only one who completely fit in, adjusting to our idiosyncrasies and becoming an integral part of the family. Stephanie literally became another sister. She lived with us for many years and received an education. To this day we share fond memories of our time together. She now holds a doctoral degree.

The same summer that Stephanie came to live with us I was preparing to return to college in Michigan. Two weeks before my departure, Maman asked me to go shopping with her. Since I needed to purchase some items for school, I gladly went along. When we reached the store, she went directly to the linen department. She was selecting sets of sheets and towels and toiletries, along with other things. Since I didn't need any linens, and I knew that she wasn't buying them for my siblings, I asked, "Maman, why are you buying linens? I don't need any of these." (It was my third year in college)

She hesitantly responded, "There are two young ladies coming to stay with us. They are coming from another country, and they will attend school in Montreal."

I asked her, "When did you find out about this?"

"Recently," she replied.

"When are they arriving?" I continued.

"Tomorrow morning," she muzzled.

"Oh no!" I exclaimed. "Papa has turned our home into an inn. Where are we going to place them? We already have two ladies here. He is doing it again, and you're letting him get away with it. It's easy for him to bring people in our home whenever he wants to without consulting us. He is gone during the day, and you have to deal with these people. Enough! You've got to stop this, Maman. Whose room are you using this time?"

"Evangeline and Jasmine's room."

I was floored. The girls were not aware that plans were being made to invade their private domain.

I warned, "Wait until Rosie and the others hear about this!"

Maman didn't say too much.

We went home after shopping for the newcomers. I couldn't wait to reach home and tell the girls. When I did, they hit the ceiling. They all went into a rampage worse than I did in the store. We felt sorry for Maman though. She was miserable whenever we were collectively upset at Papa. She would not stand for it and defended him furiously. We felt that Maman indulged him too frequently. Since we had no intention to upset her, we stopped complaining, and in spite of our state of displeasure, we helped her set up the room. But we were waiting until Papa came home!

Maman tried to pacify us before Papa arrived home. She tried to make us feel guilty, but it didn't work this time. She tried to call on our obligation to observe the fifth commandment, which is to "honor thy father and thy mother." She also reminded us that there was a promise attached to that command. We assured her that we had no intention of disrespecting Papa; we wouldn't dare try even if we wanted to. However, we needed to express our sentiments regarding this recurring issue.

By the time Papa came home, everyone was calm. No one seemed willing to talk to him about it because we felt that it would have been futile anyway. But I wasn't about to let it go this time. So I talked to him alone. I calmly approached him and shared my concern with him. I suggested that he allow us to participate in the decision-making process, since we are so intimately involved.

He looked at me and said, "Ma fille, there are times when I have to make decisions instantly. I don't have the luxury of time to consult anyone. As the head of this house, I have to make decisions based on my conviction. These are two young ladies who are in dire need of help. They have a great need to be away from their home. There are times when I have to make decisions even when I know that I will encounter resistance from my family. Trust me to do the right thing. You may not understand now, but you will. I beg you; please work with your mother to make their stay comfortable."

I thought, *Here he goes, trying to put a guilt trip on me.*

It didn't work this time, but it seemed futile to continue the conversation. He was the parent after all. Papa always knew that we would eventually accept his decisions and would be kind to our guests no matter how displeased we may have been.

The next day they arrived from the airport with Papa. We were cordial and helpful. Luckily, I was scheduled to leave for college shortly thereafter. Danielle and Janine were first cousins. Janine was helpful in the kitchen. She set the table and washed the dishes after meals. However, Danielle never participated. Strangely, Janine always buttered Danielle's bread and cut her food. Janine was always by her side at the dining table. I didn't give it a second thought. After all, my sisters and I did things for each other all the time.

I returned home for Christmas vacation to find that our guests were quite comfortable. One day I planned to go shopping in downtown Montreal, and Danielle asked to come along. We traveled on the metro. On our way home, I was sitting on the opposite seat facing her. Inadvertently, my eyes rested on her right hand. It looked so different, almost dead. I looked at her two hands, and they looked different. Then I realized that her right hand was prosthesis. I froze.

She saw the look on my face and said, "Is this the first time you've noticed it?"

I said nothing because I didn't know what to say. She quickly proceeded to tell me the whole story. I listened in horror about what happened to this seventeen-year-old young lady.

Danielle's church had planned a picnic at the beach. Her mother had no plans to attend the picnic but allowed her to go with relatives and friends. Prior to her departure, Danielle's mother reminded her to exhibit proper Christian behavior. She was warned specifically not to swim even if everybody else did. She reluctantly agreed to obey her mother's command. Danielle left, intending to have a wonderful time.

The picnic was great fun. Danielle was enjoying her time with her friends. Sometime in the afternoon, a shark was seen near the beach area where everyone was swimming. Someone screamed, "Shark in sight! Shark in sight! Everyone get out of the water!"

Danielle, knowing that her best friend, Yvette, was swimming, rushed to find her. She began to look for her, but to no avail. She asked others about her, but no one could locate her. Some people mentioned that the last time they saw her she was in the water. Danielle began to panic.

Before the warning about the shark, most of the people were swimming near the bank, but Danielle thought that Yvette might have gone out further. She was one of the few who could swim well. Danielle was afraid that something might have happened to her friend, so she decided to go into the water to look for her.

She started swimming farther away from the people, looking for Yvette. As she was swimming, she saw the shark and tried to avoid it by dipping in the water. Unfortunately, the shark saw her and moved rapidly toward her. This time she was swimming to save her life. As she reached the shore, she looked back and saw a trail of blood behind her. She looked at her body and noticed that her right arm was cut off. Danielle didn't notice that when the shark passed by her rapidly, its fin cut her arm on the upper mid section. She fainted at the sight of this horror.

Danielle was immediately transported to the hospital. They tried to retrieve her arm from the sea, but to no avail. As a result a prosthesis was attached to her upper arm. She was eleven years old. At every growth spurt, adjustments were made in order to fit the prosthesis to match her new size. "What happened to your friend Yvette?" I asked her.

She responded, eyes engulfed with tears, "She was fine. When she saw the shark from a distance, she hurried out of the water."

I was petrified. *What a tragedy!* I thought. I had heard about this horrible story, but I never dreamed that the young lady would sit right before me. I was filled with love and compassion for her. I wondered why she was in my home. Then I started to get a sense of what my father was referring to when he told me, "You will understand."

Danielle said to me, crying, "My life was completely shattered because I tried to help Yvette. Even she abandoned me like everybody else."

I told her that her friend was very young and may not have known how to handle the situation.

"Maybe," she responded.

I was moved by the whole experience and tried hard to suppress my tears. What do you say in the face of such a tragedy? Why didn't Papa and Maman prepare us for this? Although this accident occurred years before, Danielle had not recovered emotionally. She was still suffering. She stopped attending church and didn't want to have anything to do with God. The older she was, the more problematic she became to her mother. She had a turbulent adolescence. Papa's reputation as a hospitable man of God preceded him, and Danielle's mother heard of him. As a single mother, she needed help. Danielle needed to get away for a while in order to deal with these issues and get an education. That's how Danielle came to my house.

Out of these experiences, my siblings and I developed a hospitable attitude. Now, as adults, we welcome guests in our homes with open arms. I have an open-door policy. It would be a rare situation that would cause me to turn away someone in need. I have become my mother.

Besides being a pastor, my husband, Baldwin, expresses some characteristics that my father exhibited when I was growing up at home. One of them is the spirit of hospitability. We have had so many occasions where we, too, exhibited deeds of hospitality. It began a year after we got married.

We had just moved into a new apartment with our firstborn son, who was one month old. One Wednesday evening Baldwin went to prayer meeting at church. He called me from there to talk to me about a young man, Thomas, who had come to the states from Africa to go to school. He was depleted of all funds and had to live in a shelter. He had to leave the premises early in the morning and was not permitted to return before 8:00 p.m. He was looking for a job, but it was difficult. He couldn't get assistance because he had no address. He came to church to ask for assistance.

Thomas asked if a member of the church would be willing to assist him by providing him with a room in their home until he could find a job and get a place of his own. No one responded to his request. Baldwin talked to Thomas and offered him the empty room in our small apartment. That's when he called me to find out if it was all right. I was not pleased that he had called me after offering the room to Thomas. I told him that it was not acceptable for him to make such a decision without my input.

Baldwin apologized, and I said, "Bring him home. I'll prepare the room for him." This sounded too familiar. I was reliving my childhood. Thomas lived with us for six months. He saved money, secured an apartment, and enrolled in school. Eventually, he completed his studies and got married. He was forever grateful, and we were fulfilled for having made a difference in someone's life.

On another occasion, a battered young woman ran away from her husband and went to a shelter. They didn't have enough room to take her in. Seeing her desperate condition, my sister who worked at the shelter asked if we were willing to take her in. We did.

She was so traumatized that she couldn't even speak. After the first few days of speechlessness following her arrival at our house, she began to trust us and finally shared her story with us. Her husband continuously physically and sexually abused her. She had a broken rib. He treated her as a slave in the house and wouldn't allow her to stay in touch with her family. She finally got enough courage to leave him, but she was afraid to get caught. She said that if he caught her he would kill her.

We helped her recuperate and get her strength back. Baldwin, a trained chaplain, knew how to interact with people in trauma. Two weeks later, she decided to move south and live with a relative that her husband did not know about. We bought her a one-way bus ticket, and she left. A few weeks later, we received a letter from her thanking us for being the good Samaritans on her way. She was in therapy and was on her way to recovery, safe from her abusive husband. She said that she would never forget our act of love and kindness toward her. She wrote, "You are angels God put in my way to help me. Thank you."

I understood why Papa did not turn others away. The feeling of joy and satisfaction I get from helping others is beyond words.

I have gone as far as taking in a family of six for three months. My girlfriend was in need of a place to live while going through the process of purchasing her home. This process was complicated and lengthy. She and her family—husband, wife and four children—had resorted to sleeping in a tent. When I heard of it, I invited the family to come and live with us until they could move into their new home. When they resisted, I would not take no for an answer. They moved in. Fortunately, our house was spacious enough to have them comfortably live with us for three months. Sound familiar? It's as though Baldwin and I were walking on the same road that Papa and Maman walked before. Incredible!

I find that this society is losing its sense of hospitality. We are so busy amassing wealth that we don't even take time to invite others for dinner in our home. We trust no one, and we live in fear. I cannot tell others to imitate what my parents, Baldwin, and I have done, because God has given each of us different gifts. But to those whom He gives the gift of hospitality, He expects them to utilize it gladly for the benefit of others. By example, Papa and Maman taught us about hospitality, compassion, and caring for others. They sometimes supplied the needs of others even at the expense of their own needs. I have learned to emulate my parents, and the very thing that I resisted I now embrace with pleasure. I am enriched by serving others in this manner. To this, Papa would say, "Benit soit l'Eternel!"

TEN

WORLD OF POSSIBILITY

Papa's life was the personification of Hebrews 11:1, which states, "Faith is the confidence that what we hope for will actually happen; it gives us assurance about things we cannot see" (NLT).

His faith was so deep that he believed that whatever he needed, prayed for, or declared in the name of Jesus had been fulfilled and would be manifested at the appropriate time. He received responses to requests all the time, and sometimes even beyond his expectations.

He believed that true faith must be active. He was so confident that his requests were granted that he behaved as though they were already acquired. He was in a place where he made declarations and without a shadow of a doubt believed that they would come into existence. I witnessed him, at myriads of occasions, declare impossible things and see them materialize.

Baldwin, my husband, says that, "God gave us the power to speak what is as though it already was such that it is." That is faith!

Papa taught us to practice that kind of faith. His greatest desire for his children was to see us develop trust and profound faith in God. He taught us that when we live in God's will, whatever we ask of Him, we will receive. We can speak boldly and expect it to happen.

Papa practiced active faith. He continuously spoke his needs into existence. When he spoke, his faith never wavered. Sometimes I asked in amazement, "What kind of faith does this man have?"

When he prayed, he seemed fixated on the end results, never considering other alternatives. I fearfully thought, *What if he does not get what he asked for?* But there was no such question with Papa. He trusted God implicitly. I observed him in situations where he prayed, got up from his knees, and literally started speaking and acting as though the object of his request had already come to fruition. At times he declared something to happen, and to my amazement, it happened. Words from his mouth became life in his hands right before our very eyes. He made faith palpable for me. At the conclusion of each instance of faith, he uttered with laughter in his voice, "Gloire a Dieu! Benit soit L'Eternel!" (Glory be to God! Blessed be the Lord!)

By watching him, I developed the expectation that when my father asked for something, sooner or later it would appear. In fact, when I needed something, I would go to Papa so that he would pray for me. I was certain that if he asked for it, I would definitely receive it. All of us developed that same expectation. As my siblings and I grew older, Papa would lament about our seemingly lack of connection with God. He felt that we relied too much on him to reach God.

One morning at family worship, he declared, "If my presence prevents you from developing a close relationship with God, if I am in the way between you and God, then let God take me so that you can experience Him for yourselves." I was immediately afraid that he would die, because when Papa spoke, things happened. His greatest desire was for his children to develop a close relationship with God. He wanted us to trust and rely on Him completely. He lived a certain way so that we would emulate him. The many instances of faith that I witnessed should have caused me to develop a profound faith in God. But because such faith was commonplace, we took things for granted. If my father said it would happen, it would happen. I had faith in my father's faith. That was good enough for me. I believed that God had answered my prayers. Papa's concern was valid, for I recall praying one time to the God of my father.

My transformation of faith in God occurred while traveling to Lincoln, Nebraska, at 18 years of age.

Three years prior to moving to Nebraska, my mother, older sister, and I relocated from New York to Boston, Massachusetts. When we first left Haiti, we stayed in New York for eight months. Papa matriculated at Union College in Lincoln, Nebraska, to complete his college education, and my other six siblings remained in Haiti with relatives. The fragmentation of the family was very trying and challenging for us. This was one of the sacrifices that our family had to make in order to survive and reach our goals. My parents felt that such a sacrifice was worth it.

My father's success up to this point in his life was not credited to formal education. He was a renowned evangelist, yet he had not earned a college degree. Although no one would know it through meeting him, his schooling ended at eighth grade. He was a self-taught man—he devoured every book in sight. He was an avid reader and became an erudite. He received credits for two years of college by passing CLEP tests without ever going to high school. His goal was to complete a doctoral degree in theology. Since Papa's education was a priority, we remained fragmented until such a time came for Papa to financially support a family of ten.

During this time of separation, my mother, older sister, and I settled into our new apartment in Boston. We had to adjust to living in a small space after having lived in spacious houses. We also had to adjust to the quiet— no talking, joking, and laughing; no arguments and fights; no talking at the same time; no commotion in my room like it was Grand Central Station. I missed chatting with my brothers and sisters; I missed singing at worship time. It was unbearable at first, especially for Maman. She couldn't bear living away from her little ones. Papa came to visit during his vacation time. He called and wrote frequently, but things were no longer the same. I cannot imagine how lonely it was for him to live alone so far away from his large family.

As time went by, I enjoyed the new lifestyle and freedom that Boston afforded. I changed from being the second oldest to the youngest in the house. I enjoyed that. I began to develop great friendships. I experienced my first love at sixteen years of age. I wouldn't have dared to even think about having a boyfriend before the age of eighteen if the family were together, because Papa wouldn't have stood for it. Papa had made the rule that the acceptable age to begin any amorous relationship was eighteen, not one day sooner. When rules were made in my home, my older sister and I were expected to obey them because we were the oldest and our younger siblings were watching and emulating us. So it was no surprise that he broke up this relationship when he found out. I was heartbroken, but I had no choice. Although Papa didn't live with us, nevertheless, he ruled the house.

After living in Boston for two and half years, Papa announced that we would be joining him in Lincoln along with the rest of the family. He made arrangements to send for my siblings and to pick us up in Boston in August. My older sister, Rosie, and I protested. We didn't want to leave our friends and the life we had become accustomed to in Boston. We suggested that Papa and the rest of the family join us in Boston instead.

Maman, however, was delighted. Finally, she was going to be rejoined with her beloved husband and all her children. I thought it was unfair to have us adjust to a new life then take it away soon after we had grown accustomed to it. I was determined to fight it until the end. I lost. The matter was not negotiable. The time for our departure was set and soon approaching. Papa was coming in two months to move us to Lincoln, Nebraska, a no-man's-land.

As a pastor's family there was no sense of stability because we moved very frequently. Moving had taken place so many times before. It didn't seem to matter as much before because we were younger and unexposed. I didn't make too many friends before. My world revolved around my family. This time I had friends to whom I was attached, and I wasn't about to be separated from them. After all, I was eighteen! Friends were more important to me than breathing. This was the first time that I had developed close relationships. In the past I had few. I was told that my large family was enough for me. My father always told us that we didn't need to have friends outside of the family because there were enough of us to make up for all the friends we wanted.

Another reason for my distress was the freedom factor. I realized that once the family reunited the freedom to do as I pleased would be stripped from me. As an older child, I was expected to be a certain way because I was the example. I was not prepared to take on such a responsibility at this stage of my life. My father and I constantly disagreed on various issues. While Papa was gone, I exercised my power of choice. Moving back together meant that I had to submit once we were together again. I had a lot to lose.

Unfortunately, the two months passed rapidly, and once again, I was being uprooted involuntarily. Papa came home and we began the laborious task of packing. Packing was a slow and painful process for me. Going through my personal belongings was extremely torturous. I had accumulated a lot in two years. As I examined all items, I reminisced on the events that surrounded their acquisition. Some were entangled with deep and strong emotions. Others were dispensable. I saved some items and discarded others. I cried as I touched some items of clothing, read love letters and cards, and looked at pictures taken during those two years. My life was being ripped apart, and there was nothing I could do to stop it. I had to leave behind my close friends, church family, and most of all, my freedom. I was sad, angry, and help-less.

The day before we departed, I went around Boston bidding farewell to my beloved friends. We cried as we hugged once more, remembering the memorable times we'd shared. We were etching in the annals of our memories one more moment of our relation-ship. My heart tore apart with every good-bye. It was a heart wrenching experience for me. Maman was giddy and couldn't understand why we were having such a hard time. She thought that we should have been happy since the family was reuniting. I cried all night, praying and hoping that somehow a miracle would occur that would prevent us from leaving Boston.

᭐᭐᭐

The dreadful day of departure arrived. We were all packed and ready to go. At 4:00 a.m. we bid farewell to our beloved Boston and everything that was precious to us in that city. As far as I was concerned, life was over. I thought, "Who goes to Lin-coln, Nebraska, anyway?" We had never heard of this place be-fore. We knew no one there. We had to start all over again. My sister and I were angry at my father, and we expressed it emphati-cally.

It was going to be a long trip, so my parents had created an itinerary. They planned to travel all day on Friday and stop before sundown. We would rest on the Sabbath in a hotel and start driv-ing again at sundown on Saturday night. We would then arrive in Lincoln on Sunday afternoon. As much as I dreaded that long trip, I dreaded getting there even more.

As I expected, Friday was difficult. We mourned all day. Rosie and I were in agony. The atmosphere in the car was heavy. We spoke only when we had to register a complaint. Finally, when Papa had heard enough of our complaints, he made us an offer. He proposed, "I am giving you a choice. If you want to be in Boston so much, I will let you go back." My mother gave him a surprised look but said nothing. He continued, "I will give you bus fare and five hundred dollars to help you re-establish yourselves in Boston. After that, you will be independent adults. You will be responsible to take care of yourselves independent of us. Or you can choose to come with the family to Nebraska and cooperate with us. You decide what you want, it's your choice."

Of course, there was a condition attached to the offer. If we chose to stay with them, we had to put up and shut up; we had to stop whining and crying. Papa gave us some time to think it over and make our choice.

Rosie and I talked about it for a very short period of time before we made our decision. We knew that five hundred dollars would not be enough for us to maintain the lifestyle we were accustomed to, and we were not willing to work hard to earn more. We realized that we would be lost without our family, and we weren't ready to be out on a limb by ourselves. So, we reluctantly decided to go with the family to Nebraska and cooperate with Papa. When we informed him of our decision, he said, "Are you sure you had enough time to think about this?"

"Yes," we grumbled.

"You are certain that you want to give up your beloved Boston to live a dull life with this family?"

"Yes," we muttered.

"Since this is your choice, you will cooperate with your mother and me. We will hear no more grumbling and complaints. We will be pleasant and cordial to one another during the remainder of the trip. Do we have an agreement?"

"Yes."

"I have your word?"

"Yes."

"Then it's settled."

Now that I am a parent, I realize that my father employed a great strategy to settle the situation. He used the power of choice. Instead of allowing us to be the victims, he gave us the opportunity to become responsible in the matter. Once we made our choice, we were transformed. From that moment the atmosphere changed in the car. Our attitude changed. When we left Boston, there were two camps in the car: us against them. When we made our choice, we became one camp. We were still sad, angry even. And at times we whispered complaints to each other, but we had to take ownership of everything that took place, because we chose it.

I wished Papa had given us that choice while in Boston though. The outcome might have been different. Months after we left Boston, I asked Papa why he didn't give us the choice to stay while we were in Boston. He admitted that, given how committed we were to stay in Boston, he didn't want to take the chance. We might have accepted his offer. He was a wise man.

Between Saturday night and our arrival in Lincoln on Sunday afternoon, Papa stopped to make numerous phone calls. I found that odd and wondered about the nature of those calls. Every time he returned to the car, I heard him tell Maman "Not yet, but don't worry." The more he called, the more my curiosity intensified.

On one of his stops, I asked Maman, "Who is he calling so frequently?" Maman didn't respond. I thought that she didn't hear me, so I repeated the question. Once again she didn't respond. When I looked at her face, my curiosity heightened. I knew that she was intentionally withholding information from us. We insisted that she inform us about the nature of the frequent telephone calls that Papa was making. My mother proceeded to inform us that we didn't have a house to move into once we reached Lincoln.

"What?" I said in disbelief.

She continued, "Papa has not located a house spacious enough to rent. He doesn't have enough money to purchase one yet, so he is looking to rent one temporarily. Remember, we are a large family of ten. It is difficult to find a rental big enough for us."

I was stupefied. "Why did he move us from our comfortable life in Boston when he didn't have a home for us to live in Lincoln?" *I went through all this pain of separation to be homeless?* I thought.

My older sister and I bombarded Maman with all kinds of questions. "Where does he plan to take us then? How are we going to live there? What's that place like anyway? Why did he keep this important piece of information from us?"

She responded impatiently, "Look, don't start again. Your father assured me that we will have a house by the time we get to Lincoln. That's good enough for me. And it should be for you too." By then Papa was returning to the car, and in an effort to protect him from us (as she always did), Maman cautioned, "Don't give him a hard time and make things more difficult. I know you, Pollyanna," she said pointing her finger at me. "You are already here, so make the best of it. Your father has always provided for you; this time is no different." Papa returned and silence filled the car.

Suddenly, I found myself in a whirlwind of emotions. I was in a state of disbelief and disappointment over the whole situation. I felt let down by my father who always had things under control. I was sad, since I had not recuperated from mourning the loss of my friends. I was filled with apprehension as I was facing the unknown with uncertainty. Why me? I sat beside my sister, my throat engulfed and my heart wrenching with pain.

I was on the verge of speaking, but Maman broke the silence and said, "Naasson, the children are inquiring about the nature of these frequent phone calls." I had expected my father to say that this was none of our concern, since we were not the decision-makers in the family.

To my surprise, he announced, "I am calling Mr. Osberg to get the address of our new home. He is still looking." And he waited.

Remembering Maman's warning, I hesitated. Then I broke what seemed like a long silence. I had to be careful in the way I addressed the issue. Finally, I took my chance and said, "So, if you don't have a place for us to move in, why didn't you wait?"

He responded, "It is time for the family to be reunited. We have been separated for too long. It is time."

I continued, "You've been looking for a house for a while, and you haven't found one. How can you be so sure that you're going to find one today? What will you do if you don't get a house? Did God tell you to do this?"

It didn't make sense to me that a man with so much wisdom would move his family without first securing a place for them to live. I thought that because Papa missed his family so much, especially his wife, he wouldn't listen to reason. He had been obstinate in the past when he thought that God directed him to do something. But this decision seemed insane.

Maman interrupted, "That's enough!"

But Papa calmly proceeded to tell us about the events that preceded the trip. The phone calls were made to Harry Osberg who was responsible for student housing at the college. He also had access to real estate properties in town since he was connected with a number of agencies. Harry had promised Papa that when the time came for him to bring his family to Lincoln he would find him a house. Harry searched for a house as much as Papa did individually. They searched for months, but neither of them could find one.

When the time came for Papa to go to Boston to get us, Harry suggested that he wait until he secured a place. Papa told him that God had directed him to bring the family together. The family needed to be settled before the school year began. He told Harry not to worry because God had a house for him. He requested that Harry continue to look while he moved the family. Harry thought Papa was unbending and unwise, and although he didn't believe that he would find a house, he reluctantly consented to continue the search for him.

As we were approaching Lincoln, Harry grew more and more concerned for Papa and was alarmed at his unrelenting attitude. Every time Papa called Harry to inquire about the house, Harry would respond, "There's no house Naasson. Remember, I advised you to secure a house before you brought your family here."

At the end of every call, Papa told him, "Don't worry, Harry. I have a house. God has already seen to it."

We reached Omaha. We were only four hours from Lincoln. Papa called Harry again, and Harry said, "There is still no house. Listen, Naasson, I am going to reserve some rooms at a motel for you until we can figure out what to do next."

Papa encouraged him, "You don't need to do that my brother. Just keep on looking."

Harry, in exasperation, said, "When are you going to get it?" With Papa's insistence, he consented, "Alright, Naasson; it's your family."

After he returned to the car, I asked Papa, "What if you don't get a house? Aren't you concerned?"

"Ma fille, there is no worry or doubt when you are in the will of God. God can do the impossible when you have faith. With men, this is impossible. But with God, all is possible." He paused

for a moment then declared, "God's will is that my family be to-
gether. I need a house for my family to live in, and I have asked
Him for it. We will have a house when we arrive in Lincoln. The
God I serve has already provided me a house. You will see."

"So why didn't He give you one before you left Lincoln?" I
insisted.

Papa patiently responded, "Maybe because He wants to teach
you a lesson about faith."

           ◈   ◈   ◈

When we arrived in Lincoln, Papa drove directly to the college to meet with Harry. Maman said, "You're not calling him first?"

"No, it's not necessary." He assured her.

Maman showed wisdom by keeping silent. I sensed doubt and
nervousness coming from her. She must have been concerned to
have asked the question. That validated my position. I was sitting
in the car wondering if my father had lost his mind. It was unreal.
I was taught about faith, heard him preach sermons about it, and
witnessed its evidence numerous times. But never did I witness
such a level of undauntable and unwavering focus. Papa parked
the car, told us that he would return, and left. After what seemed
to be an eternity, Papa reappeared. We looked at his face to determine what happened. But his face was motionless and his hands
empty.

I thought, *He didn't get the house. I knew it.* I panicked. *What
is he going to do now?*

By then Papa had entered the car. He began driving, looking
straight ahead as to avoid looking at Maman. We all figured that
he didn't get the house. We were disappointed, especially for him.
We didn't know what to say. We didn't dare say a word but waited
for him to speak. He didn't. We drove for a few minutes. Then,
after making a few turns on some streets, he stopped, pointed at a
house, and said, "Here is our house." He pulled out a key from his

shirt pocket and showed it to us saying, "Never underestimate the power of God. We have a house. My God did it again!"

We were thunderstruck and dumbfounded. Having been in the company of my father all my life, I should have known that the situation would have resulted in this manner. I wondered what could have happened between Omaha and Lincoln that changed the situation from impossibility to reality.

When we arrived at the God-given house, Papa asked us to go in the house for prayer, so that we could thank God for providing for us in our time of need. We followed his directive and entered the house. As always, he used this event to reinforce lessons previously taught. This time it was about faith. He began to share with us the events that occurred within the last four hours.

When he entered Harry's office, he was warmly greeted. Harry's voice sounded totally different than before. Excitingly, he said, "Pastor Prosper, what kind of man are you? I need to develop your kind of faith. You wouldn't believe what just happened!"

He proceeded to tell Papa that shortly after his call from Omaha, a lady called his office. This lady was a member of his church. Strangely, he normally didn't go to his office on Sundays. She explained that she had a family emergency. She had to immediately go to California to take care of her ailing mother. However, because she was going to be in California indefinitely, she had a dilemma. She had a three-bedroom furnished house that she didn't know what to do with. Having no time, she called Harry, seeking his help to manage the property for her. Interestingly, the house also had two empty bedrooms in the basement that she used to rent to students from the college. She was leaving within a couple of hours. She asked Harry to put the furniture in storage and rent the house for her! Harry, in shock, gladly accepted the challenge. When he hung up the phone, he couldn't believe it.

"That's Naasson's house! What kind of man is this? I can't believe it! This is a miracle!" he shouted. A miracle was appropriate
because God came to Papa's rescue at a time when it seemed impossible. When God answers prayers, He leaves no room for im-
provement. There were enough bedrooms to accommodate the
whole family, two persons per room. God had indeed operated a
miracle because of my father's faith. Harry immediately got a
crew together, and in approximately three and half hours, the
house was empty, clean, and ready for us to move in. Incredible!
When Papa picked up the key, Harry confessed his lack of faith,
determined to practice Papa's kind of faith, and praised God with
him. They thanked each other, and Papa joyfully left with the keys
to his house.

When Papa finished sharing the story with us, he added, "Remember that when you are faithful to God, whatever you ask Him,
He will give it to you." He continued, "The proof is in John 14:12-
14. Jesus said, 'I tell you the truth, anyone who has faith in me
will do what I have been doing. He will do even greater things
than these, because I am going to the Father. And I will do whatever you ask in my name, so that the Son may bring glory to the
Father. You may ask me for anything in my name, and I will do it'
(NIV). I needed a house for my family. I asked God for it in the
name of Jesus, and He gave it to me. Gloire a Dieu! Benit soit
l'Eternel!" We prayed and thanked God for providing for us one
more time.

As for me, I was aghast. Boston seemed insignificant at that
moment. I was profoundly moved and inspired by the events of
the day. Although I'd witnessed faith in action numerous times before—because my parents lived a life of faith—that incident may
have been the most suspenseful, powerful, and meaningful manifestation of faith that I had experienced. I confess that I was happy
when I first heard that we didn't have a home in Lincoln. This was
the legitimate opening that I needed to return to Boston with my
family. If we couldn't settle in Nebraska, the logical thing for the

family to do would be for us to return to a familiar place, which was Boston. But Papa's faith prevailed. I was profoundly impacted by that experience. It was indeed the beginning of my walk of faith with God.

Ellen G. White states that, "As the will of man co-operates with the will of God, it becomes omnipotent" (*Christ's Object Lessons*, p. 333). When a man is committed to what he believes, God will move the universe to accommodate him. Papa had fully committed himself to believing that in the name of Jesus he had a house although the evidence proved otherwise. God shifted the universe to give him the house.

That is what faith is all about: believing fervently that I have received something I asked God for, and because of my unwavering stand, God makes it happen. I particularly appreciated my father's unwavering attitude. He never doubted, not for one minute, that God had already answered his request. I wondered, "How do I develop that kind of faith?"

The answer is in Mark 11:22-24, "Have faith in God," Jesus answered. "I tell you the truth, if anyone says to this mountain, 'Go, throw yourself into the sea,' and does not doubt in his heart but believes that what he says will happen, it will be done for him. Therefore, I tell you, whatever you ask for in prayer, believe that you have received it, and it will be yours" (NIV). Indeed, "faith is the confidence that what we hope for will actually happen; it gives us assurance about things we cannot see" (Hebrews 11:1, NLT).

I began to practice Papa's faith one step at a time. The more I practiced, the deeper my faith developed. I began to have my own experiences with God.

ॐ   ॐ   ॐ

When I got married, I wanted two children: a boy and a girl. After the birth of my second son, I still wanted my girl, but I was afraid that I might have a third boy. I was thrilled with my two boys, but I desperately wanted a girl. A year after my second son's birth, I decided that the time to have my girl had come. In order to guarantee a girl, I followed my father's example. I prayed. "I thank you God for giving me two beautiful, healthy boys. I am ready to have another child, and I would like it to be a girl this time. I ask you, in the name of Jesus, to put the right seed in me so I may have my girl. Thank you. Amen."

Within a month I was overtaken by that cursed morning sickness, and I knew that I was pregnant. When I had my sonograms, I didn't want to know the baby's gender because I desired to have my own faith experience. I was confident that inside of me was growing a beautiful, healthy girl. I never doubted for a minute that I was carrying a girl. During my pregnancy I always referred to the baby as she. My friends were concerned. They worried about my mental state in the event that I had another boy. They cautioned me to be open to the possibility that I may have another boy. I assured them that there was no mistake about it. It was a girl.

As my due date approached, my sister-in-law planned a baby shower for me. She asked me, "Polly, what is your color theme for the baby?"

"Pink, of course."

"Don't you want a neutral color just in case it's a boy?"

"I want pink for my girl."

"Ok, if you say so."

My friends grew more concerned about me when she told them of my choice of color. They tried to prepare me for the "worst," as they put it, but to no avail. My faith never wavered. I wouldn't allow them to affect me by allowing doubt to enter my mind. I remained strong. I was certain that it was a girl because I asked God for her. So all my plans centered on my girl. I was focused, just like Papa.

Labor began two weeks prematurely and delivery was induced. When the doctor held up my baby and said "it's a girl," my faith in God grew exponentially. I expected God to deliver on my words, "I have a girl." And He did.

∽ঔ   ∽ঔ   ∽ঔ

A few years ago, I was approached to apply for a position. I was told that there was a position for superintendent of schools for the Northeastern Conference headquartered in New York City, and I was the perfect person for the job. Initially, New York was not part of my future plans. I was not interested. Being persuaded to send in my résumé, I didn't expect anything to come of it since I didn't see any possibility of that happening. I thought nothing of it until I received a letter of reply, which indicated that my résumé had been submitted to the search committee and they would be contacting me if I qualified for an interview.

Realizing that the job may be a possibility, I needed to know God's will concerning the position. I needed to know if it was His will to go to New York to work as superintendent of schools. I didn't want to proceed without knowing God's plan. In November I decided to consult God. Papa wrote a book, *Seven Days with God*, in which he developed a plan that, if followed, assured a response from God. I followed the plan. My mother and sisters and I decided to pair up and have a week of prayer with the book as our manual. It was customary for Papa to ask God for a sign when he wasn't clear of God's will in a particular situation.

Similarly, when I made my request to God, I asked Him for a sign. I prayed with my partner and asked, "God, if it is your will that I work in New York City as superintendent of schools for the Northeastern Conference, give me a sign. If it is your will that I work in New York as superintendent of schools, have someone ring my doorbell and ask, 'Are you considering selling this house, because I'm interested in buying it.'" The house was not for sale, and since it was November, the chance to sell a house was not favorable.

After I prayed I decided to share my request with my husband and daughter, the only child still left at home. Months later on a Friday in the middle of winter, the ground blanketed with snow, my frenzied daughter greeted me from work with, "Mommy, Mommy, he came." She handed me a business card. "About 1:30 p.m., a man rang the doorbell. I answered, and he said, 'Are your parents home?' I told him no, and he said, 'Are they interested in selling this house? Because I'm interested in buying it.'"

The gentleman gave her his card and asked her to have her parents call him. Baldwin had reached home before me but hadn't called the man. He felt that since it was my request I should be the one to make the call. I immediately called the man who repeated the very same words that I had uttered in my prayer. He proceeded to tell me that he had moved to the area last spring but had never visited my development. That day he had the urge to drive around, in the middle of winter, and he ended up in my development for the first time. He saw my house and paused to look at it. He said that he liked it so much that he was impressed to talk to us about buying it. He asked me, "Are you considering selling your house because I'm interested in buying it?"

I replied, "I will be selling it in a few months." He asked me several questions about the house, but when he found out that the larger bedrooms were on the second floor, he told me that the house was not suitable for him because his mother-in-law could not maneuver the stairs. She needed to have a room on the first floor. The man didn't realize that he was an answer to my prayer. He had just manifested the sign for me. God answered exactly what I asked for. I didn't ask Him to sell it.

When I hung up the phone, I jumped around the house looking for Baldwin, singing, "We're going to New York. We're going to New York." Although my daughter was not happy about leaving Michigan, she admitted that God had spoken. We thanked God for answering my request so vividly, and we were more determined to live in His will.

I was assured that I had the job, and I was moving to New York. Yet, I had not been interviewed. God had given me a sign; for me, it was a done deal. From that moment on I started to arrange my affairs for the big move. New York was not my choice because I didn't want to live in such a large city. However, since the response was clear, I started to share my plans with my friends. When I went for the interview, five months after I received the sign, I walked in that room confident that the job was mine. My primary purpose for going there was to meet the people I was going to work with. Based on the result, they believed it too. I held that position for the past seven years. My only goal was to fulfill God's plan for my life.

It was not accidental that my daughter was the recipient of the sign. She needed that experience because her response to moving from Berrien Springs was the same as my response to moving from Boston. For that, I am grateful. That's how God began His work of faith with her. Interestingly, He had the same effect on her as He did on me that Sunday in Lincoln, Nebraska.

I continue to exemplify faith in action to my children because I learned so much by watching my father. Our children learn from us. It is our duty to live a life that they want to emulate. Papa exemplified faith in action to us. I emulated him, and as my faith strengthened, I, too, experienced my own miracles with God. If we remain faithful to God, nothing is impossible.

ELEVEN

UNABASHED GENEROSITY

"Whatever you do for others, do it with all your heart. Otherwise don't do it." Papa and Maman were highly generous and kind. Generosity was a principle upheld in my home. It was a way of being. Taking care of the needs of others seemed to take precedence over their needs or ours. Papa said that the spirit of generosity includes some characteristics that we needed to embody.

Firstly, he said that it was a blessing to give to others. Papa would say to us at times, "It is more blessed to give than to receive. Give with a happy heart, not grudgingly. Do it with humility and grace so that others are not left in discomfort with your gift. Don't give to people in such a way that they would want to give the gift back to you if they didn't need it. It is better not to give at all than to give grudgingly. God is not pleased when we give with such a spirit. Give with a joyful spirit."

Secondly, we couldn't give what we didn't want. He encouraged us to give what we cherished and didn't want to part with. We were taught to treat others as we wanted to be treated. He told us that that was the true spirit of generosity.

Thirdly, we had to give expecting nothing in return. Our main purpose for giving was not to receive something in return. It was to help others. Although God promises in the Bible, that if we give we shall receive, we must give from love. Expecting something leaves people feeling indebted and leaves us disappointed if we don't receive it.

Lastly, he taught us to give liberally. That is translated qualitatively and quantitatively. We should give of ourselves and our means prodigiously for the betterment of human beings. God wants us to give without reservation. Although Papa was not a rich man, he was generous with his few possessions.

One day Maman announced, "Girls, Papa is going to buy us a sewing machine, and I will teach you how to sew. When you grow older, you will make your own clothes. "

Dressmaking for six children at that time (four girls and two boys) had become an expensive endeavor. Whenever we were in need of new clothes, Maman bought some fabric and took us to the seamstress' shop where we selected an appropriate style from a catalogue, and within a few days, we were presented with the exact replica of the garment we selected. Every time we brought the finished product home, I was amazed at the result.

"How did she do that?" I would ask Maman.

"She knows how to sew."

"Do you think I can do that someday?"

"Bien sur, if you learn how to sew."

"I want to learn how to sew just like that."

"If you apply yourself, you will."

Maman was a seamstress in her own right, so when Maman announced the soon purchase of a sewing machine, I was elated. *What a splendid idea!* I thought.

I can still remember the height of excitement that I experienced at that moment. I couldn't wait to learn to sew for myself. I figured that sewing would be easy, and it wouldn't take me too long to learn the skill. After all, I had plenty of practice sewing for my dolls. I was adept at cutting paper doll clothes and making beautiful and unusual garments. However, Maman announced that it would take two months to purchase the sewing machine.

"Two months? Why do we have to wait for two months? That's a long time!

"Polly, you know that your father gets paid once a month, and the sewing machine is not factored in this month's budget. We have to be prudent. We will be able to afford the sewing machine in two months. So we have to wait."

Remembering previous incidents when I was told to wait, I gasped, "Another long wait!" I didn't understand why pastors in our churches were paid monthly. It seemed too long. "Why can't they pay him more frequently?" I would so often mutter.

In those days church pastors were paid once a month, and based on my parents' budget, they couldn't undertake such an expense without planning. Two months was the soonest they could manage it. Since Maman was a full-time homemaker, the family depended on that once-a-month check. Two months seemed like an eternity to me.

I'm not sure why I was so interested in that sewing machine because I don't recall any interest on the part of my siblings. In fact, none of them remember this incident. I do know that I was looking forward to learning how to sew.

One day Papa drove Maman downtown to select the machine. It was agreed that Papa would pick it up for her at the appropriate time. I remember counting the days until Papa would bring the sewing machine home.

In the meantime, I daydreamed about designing and making all types of clothes when I completed my training at Maman's sewing school. I looked for garments in catalogues. I made patterns out of newspapers and paper bags. My years of cutting patterns and making dresses for my dolls were about to pay off. With that kind of experience, I knew that it wouldn't take me long to learn to sew with the sewing machine.

The other reason why I was eagerly awaiting the sewing machine was because I thought that having a sewing machine would offer me the opportunity to have as many clothes as I wanted. I remember how I envied two sisters who were also pastor's daughters. These girls were my classmates. They were always dressed impeccably. It seemed as though their parents owned a garment store.

At church, they always wore beautiful clothes with matching accessories. Although we wore uniforms in school, theirs seemed to look better—the pleats crispier, the fabrics of finer quality. When our church school had special church programs, they stepped in with new dresses and beautiful hats and gloves. I compared theirs to mine, and my heart was inflamed with envy. I used to daydream about a day when I would be as finely dressed as they. The day never came. My family increased with more girls and my hope for abundance in clothes vanished. We were seven sisters.

Sharing our clothes was one of the advantages of having many sisters. Because we were close in age and size, we could wear each other's clothes. Although we didn't have too many clothes individually, we had clothes in abundance collectively. Interestingly, while I thought that we didn't have enough clothes, others thought that we had plenty. To this day, we wear each other's clothes.

We also had numerous "adopted" brothers and sisters. They were those brothers and sisters my father met along the way. If they were in need and we could help, we had to share with them. Papa gave generously. He gave his possessions and ours. I didn't like that too much. In fact, I resented Papa when he gave to others what belonged to us. I didn't think that I had enough of anything for myself, especially clothes. At least not as many as I wanted or thought I deserved. At times I thought that if my parents were less generous, I could have everything I wanted.

I asked Papa, "Why do you give so much to people while we don't have enough at home?"

And Papa would respond, "But my darling, you have enough. You have what you need."

"We could have more if it weren't for other people."

"And what would those people have if we didn't give to them? God supplies all our needs. It is our duty to help those in need. Polly, there is joy in giving."

"Joy! I don't feel joy when you give others what's mine."

"God will bless you when you share your possessions."

"Where is the blessing?" I thought.

My mother would sing, "I have two dolls, and I'm so glad. You have no dolls, and I'm so sad. Since I love you, my dear friend, I will share them with you. For this is what Jesus would have me do."

On such notes, I had nothing else to add. I felt ashamed of my selfishness and stopped whining and complaining. I consoled myself with the fact that I was touching somebody's life.

୬ଡ଼   ୬ଡ଼   ୬ଡ଼

It was the first day of the month. Papa got paid and could finally buy the sewing machine for Maman. Truthfully, I dreamt about it so much that I had taken ownership of that machine. That morning I said good-bye to Papa with great anticipation. I was excited. I asked Papa if he was going to pick up the sewing machine; he smiled at me and said "yes." I remember thinking that if I could wait for two months I could wait for one more day. I was ecstatic.

All day long I anticipated Papa's arrival. I looked at the clock continuously. Strange enough, the day seemed to go by rapidly. Customarily, Papa arrived home late in the evening. So I expected him late. However, in the late afternoon, I heard a car in the driveway. Since I wasn't expecting Papa until later, I didn't pay much attention to it. I thought it might have been someone visiting my mother.—We were taught not to show up when there was company unless we were called. We were to come in, respectfully salute the visitor(s), then disappear.—So that was not my concern. Suddenly, I heard, "Papa's home!" My heart leaped with excitement.

By the time I reached the front porch, my father was already out of the car and headed toward the trunk, surrounded by my brothers and sisters. I remember how beautiful the day was. Not a cloud in the sky. I stopped and watched him go around the back, open the door, and retrieve something that seemed heavy. I remember watching him lift the item, in slow motion, and I held my breath, waiting for the long awaited moment when this machine would be in sight.

My heart was palpitating. I could hear every heartbeat—fast, heavy, and loud. In unbearable anticipation, I felt lightheaded for a moment. My heart must have stopped when I saw my father pull out his briefcase from the car and close the door. I wondered, *Where is the sewing machine?* I was numb. I was sick with disappointment. Then I thought, "*OK. He left the sewing machine in the trunk of the car. He must be teasing my mother.*

As he came up the stairs, I approached him and kissed him. I asked, "Where's the sewing machine?" sounding disappointed.

As he bent down for me to kiss him, he asked without looking at me, "Where is your mother?" Something about his voice made me suspicious; it felt as though he didn't even notice me. I knew something went wrong.

My father entered the house, looking for my mother. I heard her say, "You're home early!" Then they disappeared into their bedroom. I contemplated the thought of listening behind the door. That thought soon perished when I considered the consequences of such an action. So I waited down the hall at a strategic place where I could see them when they came out of their room. How I wished I were a fly on my parents' bedroom wall!

After what seemed like an eternity, they reappeared. My mother was smiling, so I thought, *If she is smiling, everything must be OK.* I immediately approached them and asked, "Where is the sewing machine?"

My mother looked at my father, and my father took me by the hand and started walking toward the backyard where everyone was. "I will tell everyone what happened at the same time." I knew then that Papa did not buy the sewing machine. I became cold and angry. I was livid but quiet as I walked with my father.

We reached the back porch, and my father summoned every-one. He sat down on the lounge chair—where he usually sat in the evening to tell us stories—and he took me on his lap. Everyone was attentively waiting. He began to tell us what he thought to be a remarkable story from which we would learn another life lesson.

He began the story with his excitement at awakening on this day, the day he would bring home the sewing machine. He loved to bring us things. So I could imagine that he was happy about that. Around lunch time, he decided to pick up the machine, and he did. He decided to visit a few people that afternoon since he wanted to be home early for supper. When he completed his church responsi-bilities, he decided to visit this family on his way home.

During his visit with the family, the mother told him, "Pastor Prosper, please pray for me. You see, things have been very hard for me since my husband died. It has been increasingly difficult to take care of six children with the money I have. I am a good seamstress, but I can't afford to buy a sewing machine. If I had one, I could make clothes for people and make money to take care of my family. I'd like you to pray for me and ask God for a sewing machine."

My father agreed, and they both knelt down to pray. After the prayer, my father told her to wait a minute. He went out the house and to the car; he opened the trunk and took out *MY* sewing machine. He went back to the house and placed the sewing machine on the table and said to the lady, "My sister, God answered your prayer even before you spoke. Here's your sewing machine."

He came home overjoyed that he had touched somebody's life, yet again trusting that my mother would be mutually happy for doing such a good deed. Of course my mother was. Whatever my father did was always all right with her. He could do no wrong.

My response was different than Maman's. I was not happy! I thought, *Once again, someone else's needs supersede ours. Why do my parents have to be so generous? And worse, why does my mother have to be so accepting of it?*

Sometimes I wished that Maman would stand up to my father and let him know how unfair he was to us. But I never saw her do that. She was supportive of everything he did, and she never complained. God made Maman with His hands. While I lay in bed that night, I sobbed myself to sleep. Interestingly, my parents had no idea that the sewing machine meant so much to me. It was their project. For Papa, life was wonderful as long as my mother was satisfied.

Papa promised Maman that he would buy another sewing machine the following month. She smiled to acquiesce. I asked, "Why didn't you give the lady a sewing machine next month?" My father looked at me, and with a solemn voice, he answered,

"When God gives you an opportunity to help someone in need, you never hesitate." He stressed the three last words.

"Why do we always have to give? Doesn't God know our needs too?"

Papa responded, "God takes care of our needs, but He does not have to take care of our wants. My children, it is more blessed to give than to receive."

I thought, *I'd love to be on the receiving end right now.* However, I didn't dare utter those words out loud. I knew that there was nothing I could say that would make a difference. That was the end of the conversation. But I thought to myself, *I wish God would tell someone to do something over here. When our parents will be through giving our things away, we'll have nothing left.*

Well, we did get the sewing machine the following month, but it didn't matter as much. I learned to sew; however, I have no recollection of what happened after its arrival. My parents continued to give generously, expecting nothing in return. They gave things over and over, opened our home to people, and never complained. Contrary to my feelings, to them, doing good for others was their duty. They felt privileged. One of my father's sayings was, "It is an honor to help my fellow man."

As for me, the more they gave, the more determined I was to take care of myself and my own first. *Others will benefit from surplus*, I thought. I resolved that when I had children they would not be secondary in my life because I frequently felt that other people were more important to my father. I felt that his children should be his priority and he should let others fend for themselves. In the face of someone in need, my father caught amnesia. It seemed that nothing else mattered (not even his family) until that need was met. I felt that other people were taken care of at my expense. It seemed to have occurred as long as I can remember.

❦   ❦   ❦

Years later, my family experienced the Lord's provision while living in Lincoln. My father was back in school, and I was fresh in college. In order to provide for my eight siblings—six sisters and two brothers—Papa cleaned a restaurant in the middle of the night when the restaurant was closed. Maman helped; sometimes the whole family helped. My older sister had a job, and the rest of us were in school.

We lived in a big house, which my parents owned, and we owned a station wagon. Our bills were paid. We ate well, dressed decently, and were healthy. People could not comprehend how our large family survived while Papa was attending school full time. Yet, we were living fairly well, and more importantly we were happy and closely knit. Every member of the family attests that that period was the best time of our life together.

People asked Papa, "Pastor Prosper, how do you do it? How can your large family survive while you study full time?"

He always responded with a smile on his face. "The Lord provides."

As an adult with a family of three children taking care of my financial responsibilities, I still wonder how my parents made it. We were taken care of and others benefited as well. I am amazed at what my father did for us with limited means.

Then one day Papa became seriously ill. He inhaled carbon monoxide from his car while driving from California to Nebraska over a three or four day period. He suffered severe complications and stayed in the hospital for a long time. When he came home, he was bedridden for a while longer.

Papa was the main provider, and as such, he knew that it was his responsibility to take care of his family. Without his job, there wasn't enough money to manage the expenses. Although I worked on campus for about ten hours per week, the money was directly placed on my student account, so I wasn't contributing financially in the home. With the exception of my older sister, my other brothers and sisters did not contribute either. Papa reluctantly asked Maman to secure employment to earn money for the household expenses. However, my mother and my sister's incomes did not suffice to take care of the family's needs. The family was facing challenging days ahead.

Papa was popular in town. The news of his illness spread all over. What happened next changed the rest of my life. People started bringing all kinds of things to the house. They brought boxes of food: canned, boxed, fresh, and frozen. They brought clothes, shoes, boots, and coats, all brand new. They brought money, linens, kitchen utensils, and household items. They brought things we needed and things we didn't need. They were neither leftovers nor garage sale items. They were new items, some with sales tickets attached to them.

People came to visit us day and night. They inquired about our needs; they genuinely wanted to take care of our needs. Sometimes we came home and found bags of groceries on the front porch waiting for us. We got checks in the mail continuously.

One day the doorbell rang. I went to answer it, but no one was there. I looked around, and there by the door was a huge box. We carried it inside and found all kinds of things in it. Along with the items of clothing was an envelope. There was a note with a check. The note said, "We love you, and we're praying for you." There was no name. We were all overwhelmed by the level of generosity that the people extended to us.

At a time when communities in America were infested with racism and prejudice, a small community of Seventh-day Adventists in Lincoln, Nebraska, who were predominantly white, expressed true love, genuine concern, and unabashed generosity toward a foreign black family. They were Seventh-day Adventists from Union College, the college church, the community church, and the Allon Chapel Church. They were loving and caring people. I was speechless.

Every day we rushed to the hospital to share with Papa about the people's acts of generosity and love. Every time we told him about a new delivery, he responded, "Benit soit L'Eternel!" (Blessed be the Lord!)

All of us children were having a field day with the gifts. It felt like Christmas morning. We never owned so much in our life. We stored things everywhere in the house. We received new clothes that lasted for years; food that lasted months; games and toys that we never knew existed; and money that paid the bills for more than six months until my father recuperated and returned to work. Papa didn't work for six months, but he didn't lose his job. Papa recuperated.

Upon arriving at home, we showed him all the things that people had given us. He praised God and said to us, looking at me directly, "Do you remember when we were in Haiti? Do you remember all the things we gave away? I remember some people who were not happy about sharing their belongings with others. I remember some people who felt it was unfair that they should be deprived of what belonged to them. You see, we were storing them up for this time. God put all that in a bank, and He cashed them in for us in our time of need."

He continued with these biblical words, "Give, and it will be given to you. A good measure, pressed down, shaken together, and running over, will be poured into your lap. For with the measure you use, it will be measured to you" (Luke 6:38, NIV). Then he concluded with, "Always be generous. Always be merciful to the needy. And God will always provide for you."

I remembered those words. They became my motif for living. I believe that this experience was created for me to teach me a lesson for a lifetime. I learned the lesson, and I thank God for teaching it to me at an early stage of my life. I was moved by the outpouring expression of love of our community. Whenever the opportunity comes, I give generously. Not only do I give material resources, I also give of myself—my time, my God-given gifts, my hospitality, my compassion, and most of all, my love—and I give it all generously.

I once heard Oprah Winfrey say, "Never be less than generous." That's how I live because my father exemplified it for me. Whenever he got the call, he never hesitated to respond generously and joyfully. He was the personification of unabashed generosity. He always touched somebody's life. He never left people the same way he found them. Now that I am older, I see how Papa's spirit of generosity impacted my life. I, too, don't hesitate when I hear the call, and I do it joyfully and passionately. I frequently experience satisfaction and fulfillment when I generously give of myself. I have learned to understand that "it is better to give than to receive."

TWELVE

SEX AND
SELF-ESTEEM

If I had to give credit to one person for the way I view myself, it is my father. From childhood my sisters and I were the recipients of Papa's compliments. Whenever we dressed up, he would say, "Regardez mes filles. Comme elle sont belles!" (Look at my daughters. How beautiful they are!) I felt good about myself. He used to buy us pretty things like clothes, hats, gloves, etc., to which I credit my love for shopping, especially for hats. He always admired us before we left the house, especially when we were going to church. He either objected or complimented us.

As much as I loved to receive his compliments, I disliked hearing him tell me to change an outfit because it was inappropriate (too short, too tight, too revealing, etc). I remember when the long skirt returned in the 70s, right after the miniskirt madness. Rosie and I bought long gray skirts. When Papa saw us he exclaimed, "At last, the designers came up with a style I like. How wonderful!"

In spite of Papa's frequent absences, he was home for the most important phases of my life, and he paid extra attention to our needs. Although annoying at times, it felt good to know that he was paying close attention to my siblings and me.

One summer during this time period, we were in California. Papa had left early one morning, expecting to return at 5:00 p.m. to pick me up for the evening evangelistic meeting where Papa worked as coordinator of the Bible workers. It was a scorching hot summer day.

Around 3:40 p.m. I began getting ready. Papa was very punctual, and I didn't want him to wait on me. As I stepped out of the tub to reach for my towel, the bathroom door opened. I turned around to see my father opening the door. I was completely naked. Our eyes met as he said, "I'm sorry. The door was not closed. I thought you were in your room." He then immediately closed the door. That incident must have lasted a few seconds, but it felt like a long time. I was mortified. I wouldn't undress around my sisters, much less around my father. I rushed to prepare myself despite my embarrassment.

At five o'clock, Papa asked me, "Are you ready?"

I responded, "Oui," while avoiding his eyes. We left for the meeting place without uttering a word to each other. The ride to the civic center seemed longer than usual, stretching the agonizingly awkward silence with each passing city block. He tried to ask me a question or two, but the tension only thickened. The ride home was the same. As soon as we entered the driveway, I muttered, "I am tired. I am going to bed. Bonne nuit!" I raced into the house, went to my room, and quickly undressed for bed.

Shortly after, there was a knock at the door. I responded, "Come in." Papa asked if we could talk. I reluctantly agreed as he sat on the foot of the bed.

"Are you being distant because of what happened in the bathroom this afternoon?" I did not respond. He continued, "When I came in this afternoon, I went straight to the bathroom. The door wasn't completely closed, so I entered without knocking, thinking that you were in your room. I know that you expected me later, but I decided to come early. I'm sorry that I intruded on your privacy. That was not my intention. Pardonne-moi."

I responded, "There is no need to forgive you. It was an accident."

"Are you all right now? Is everything all right between us?"

"Yes. Everything is fine."

"Good."

After a quick hug and goodnight kiss, I expected him to get up and leave. But he continued, "Tell me, why are you so uncomfortable? After all, I am your father. Let's talk about it. What are you ashamed of?"

I was surprised that he posed that question because he hit the nail on the head. What should I tell him? Should I open up or lie? It's as though Papa saw through me. I was ashamed of my body. "I hate my body. I wish I looked different."

"Ma fille, you have a body that will be the envy of many women. Tu es formidable! What is it about your body that you hate?"

"I hate everything, my wide hips, and my big derriere."

"Quoi?" he smiled with great surprise. "These are great features of a black woman's body. You are shapely. You are beautiful. God made a masterpiece when he created you. Don't be ashamed of God's creation. You are a beautiful young lady."

"You are my father. You're supposed to say that." As embarrassed as I was at that moment, I was grateful to him for affirming me. Teenagers are absorbed with their self-image and at sixteen years old, I constantly doubted myself. Papa said exactly what I needed to hear. Although I didn't believe that I was beautiful, his words made a lasting impression on me.

From then on when I looked at myself in the mirror, I questioned, "Could there be some truth to what Papa said?" I remembered Papa's words of affirmation and dismissed the negative thoughts about myself. Because he constantly affirmed me, I began to think that I didn't look as bad as I initially thought. I started to look at myself positively, and this led me to act differently. Eventually, I developed confidence in myself, and I don't remember ever having a problem with my self-mage after that time, just because my papa said that I was beautiful.

One day our topic of discussion was sex. Unlike most cases where mothers talk to their daughters about sex, Papa was the first person who discussed sex with me. He talked to me about appropriate comportment with men, especially before marriage. When he started talking about inappropriateness in touching, I froze. I couldn't understand why I reacted that way. I just knew that I felt overwhelmingly uncomfortable. Papa must have sensed my reaction as well because he stopped talking. That feeling stayed with me for a while until I remembered that there was a man who touched me inappropriately when I was eight years old. I'd suppressed the memory until Papa's conversation.

The man was frequently in our home. When Papa was away preaching, he was the one who watched out for the family. If there was an emergency and Papa was unreachable, he was the one Maman contacted. There would have been no reason to believe that this man (almost a father) would abuse me.

The funny thing is that he was never inappropriate in my own home. It occurred in his house. There were not many occurrences; I only remember two distinct incidents. One time Mother sent me to his home to run an errand, and another time, my visiting cousins, siblings, and I were at his house for dinner. He inconspicuously led me to his room where he touched me, squeezed me, and said things to me which made me uncomfortable. I pulled away from him and ran home. I felt very strange, uncomfortable, and

114 In the Name of My Father

confused when he touched me. I sensed that his actions were inappropriate. I was a child, and I didn't know anything about sex. That was never discussed with me before. I wasn't sure whether I should tell my parents or not. I decided not to tell my parents, but I resolved to never be in his presence alone. I dreaded being around him and avoided him like a plague.

I was elated when, at ten years old, my father sent me away to boarding school with my older sister. I never had to see him again as a little girl. Although it hurt me to leave my family behind, the desire to never see that man again was stronger. I was happy to be out of that town. Luckily, my father was transferred to another church in another city, and I never returned. I never heard my parents mention his name again nor did he ever visit us.

I was curious to know how Papa found out about it. He claimed that I told my grandmother about it, which I didn't and still don't remember doing, but how else would she have known? In retrospect, I can see why I would have chosen her to share this secret with. My grandmother was a bold, confident, intelligent, fearless, and feisty woman. When she set her mind on something, nothing could stand in her way. She was unstoppable. She only had two sons and would not allow anyone to tamper with her family and would attempt anything to protect her young. Well, she wasn't about to let anyone hurt her little granddaughter. She was fearless, and I admired her spunk. Knowing her, she must have had some serious confrontation with him. Either way, when Grande-mère found out, she told Papa about it.

Papa confessed that this episode was one of the hardest things he ever had to deal with. He said that he experienced anger, pain, and hurt at the same time. He was angry at his friend's betrayal. He couldn't conceive that someone, especially his friend, could treat his innocent daughter that way. He was aching for me having to go through this experience, and he felt worse for not having been there to protect me. He asked God to intervene and assist him so that he would know how to handle the situation.

As we sat together on the couch, Papa said, "He was a sick man to have committed such a crime." There was no such thing as "children's rights," so Papa must have taken care of it his own way. It seemed to have been very difficult for him, because he ended the conversation without telling how he handled it, and I did not ask.

Papa took advantage of this opportunity to ensure that I was not emotionally damaged. I opened up and shared my feelings about it. It was the first time I had discussed this experience with anyone. I wondered why he chose me. I remember people saying that I was a pretty little girl. Was it something about me that attracted him to me? It was confusing to me as a child. I don't remember experiencing anger, shame, or embarrassment. As a little girl, I felt very uncomfortable about this man's behavior. It didn't feel right.

Papa said, "You did nothing wrong. Do you understand? Nothing about you made him do this. His behavior was wrong, not yours." I was grateful that we had this discussion. By the end of the long discussion, that chapter of my life was finally over. I was healed.

Years later, when I visited a church in New York, I saw the man who had touched me. I froze for a minute. Then, I relaxed and looked at him from a distance, and suddenly I felt pity for him. I remember saying to myself. "I wonder if he realizes how sick he is." Then I walked away. When I heard of his death years later, I felt relieved.

The session we had that night in California impacted me profoundly. It relieved me of any unfounded burden and cleansed me of any emotional or psychological harm. My self-esteem was boosted a hundredfold. I am so appreciative of the way Papa showed wisdom, gentleness, and sensitivity in this situation. Because of his love, the recollection of this vignette of my life has had no emotional hold on me. It's just the memory of something that happened to me a long time ago. For this, I am grateful.

When I talked to my daughter about sex and appropriateness with men— she was much younger than sixteen—I decided to share this experience with her. As my father did, I turned every opportunity into a learning moment with my children. I thought that it was a poignant way to illustrate a point, so we talked about it.

She was shocked to hear about my experience. She said, "Mom, I'm sorry that it happened to you. He was a bad man. Are you OK? I am glad that you are. Thanks, Ma, for sharing" She was appreciative that I shared this part of my past with her.

Sharing this experience with her provided another opportunity for openness and closeness between us. We have developed an open relationship with each other. She knows that I am available to discuss anything with her, making sure that she is comfortable enough to come to me or her dad about anything, just as I could with Papa and Maman.

THIRTEEN

MEN AND RELATIONSHIPS

Early one summer when Papa came to visit during a school break, he had a solemn conversation with my older sister, Rosie. Rosie had just turned eighteen, and Papa officially gave her permission to start dating the male species. Papa had a rule that no one in the house could engage in an amorous relationship with the opposite sex before the age of eighteen—we could have friends but no exclusive male friends. He said that we needed to be more mature to undertake the responsibilities that came with exclusive relationships. Furthermore, we were not allowed to date even when we had reached the age of eighteen. Our boyfriends were allowed to visit us at home in the company of an adult. Activities outside of the house were considered family outings.

Papa told Rosie, "I have been observing you, and I am pleased with the level of maturity you have displayed. You have developed into a beautiful and responsible young lady. That's why I wanted you to wait." He cautioned her, "You can never be too careful." He set some new rules and sent her on her merry way.

At that time Papa and I had a wonderful relationship. Papa used to comment on how mature I was. When I heard him talk to my sister, I figured that since I was so mature he would endorse my undisclosed relationship with my boyfriend too, although I was only sixteen. He could make an exception because of my maturity and readiness. I was so sure that he would approve that I decided to inform him of the relationship I had already begun with a young man. I moved forward with my brilliant idea and told Papa about my boyfriend. Good sense should have told me not to share that secret with him, but I was suffering from temporary insanity.

Papa was quiet for a moment, and then he said, "I am very disappointed in you. You disobeyed me. I cannot take this lightly at all."

I realized, a moment too late, that I had just committed a fatal mistake. Papa commanded me to sever the relationship immediately. I tried to reason with him, but to no avail. I tried to help him understand that we weren't doing anything wrong. I reminded him of what he had previously said to me, "But you said that I was mature and responsible. Papa, you can trust me." I tried to appeal to his emotions by saying, "But Papa I love him, and he loves me. You can trust me."

When I said those words, he was more resolved to have me end the relationship. He commanded without emotion, "Tomorrow morning you are going to put an end to this."

I was crushed. I felt that my own father didn't trust me. Now he wanted to humiliate me and ruin my life. How could he be so cruel to me? I felt that he should have taken into account that I opened my heart to him and told him the truth. Why would he want to tear my world apart? What would life be like without the love of my life? I couldn't imagine it. I had already planned our life together: we would complete high school together, then college, then finally get married and have babies. Now my father wanted to destroy all that! I couldn't let that happen. Once again, I appealed to him. "He is from a good family. You know his family."

"No."

So I resorted to insults, "But Papa, this rule is for Haiti. You are in the United States. There is a different culture here. It doesn't matter anymore. I don't see why I have to break it up."

The more I pleaded, the more resolved Papa became. "Tomorrow you break it off. C'est final."

Since Papa was leaving in the morning for California to work with Evangelist E. E. Cleveland, I decided not to break up with my boyfriend. Little did I realize that he was as powerful in his absence as he was in person. He followed up on it. He called the day after his departure, "Did you do what I asked you to do?"

"Nooooo, not yet" I said.

He was livid. "You break it off at once." The tone of his voice intensified, "I will have to get in touch with his parents."

I took a chance to voice my opinion, "You can tell his parents to keep their son away from your daughter, but what if your daughter won't stay away from him?" I went too far.

The very next day my mother received a telegram from Papa. He was too mad to speak. It said, "Put Pollyanna on a plane to Oakland tomorrow. I will call tonight to get the details of her arrival."

I protested, but Maman said, "Your father wants you there; you have to go."

I went into a tirade, "It's not fair. I could have kept on lying to him and he would have known nothing, but I had to open my big mouth. Look where honesty got me. He is punishing me for telling him the truth. I can't believe this."

Meanwhile, my mind was racing, trying to figure out what I could do to escape from the situation without making things worse. It was customary, in those days, for Haitian parents to ship their behaviorally challenged children back to Haiti to be disciplined and trained by relatives. They were exiled there, not to be seen again, in some cases, for years. I didn't want their fate, but I didn't want this break up either. I tried to fight it, but my mother wouldn't go against my father. Regrettably, I had no choice. Maman and Rosie helped me pack that evening.

Sitting on the plane early the next morning, I was devastated. I didn't even have the chance to say good-bye to my sweetheart. I was heartbroken. I sat there staring out the window; my head was as heavy as a ton of bricks; my cheeks were covered with tears and I had a runny nose, but I didn't bother to wipe my face. My body was trembling out of anger and fear. I had no idea what was ahead of me, but I knew what I left behind; I ached to be home with my love.

Inconsolable, I resolved to make him pay for tearing my world apart. *I will not talk to him. I will be mad all the time. I will be uncooperative. I will make life so miserable for both us that he will have to send me back to Boston. Then, I will have my life back just as I wanted it.* I replaced my tears with a new hope as the plane landed.

I was surprised and completely caught off guard when Papa greeted me at the gate with a big smile on his face. I was expecting to see a mad man waiting for me. I didn't know how to react to him this way. I thought, *I guess you should be the one smiling because you won. You may win the battle for now, but I will win the war later.* I kissed him while we embraced each other as is customary.

The ride "home" was tense. Papa asked me insignificant questions, and I responded with one-word answers. There seemed to be long pauses between topics. Then he must have gotten the idea that being my tour guide would fill the silence. So he proceeded to tell me about Oakland. Out of respect, I pretended to be enthusiastic exclaiming, "Ah! Really? Wow! I didn't know that. That's interesting!"

For the next couple of weeks, we were civil to each other. Then my defenses began to break down. We had casual talks, visited places, went shopping, went to church, etc. We went to the evangelistic meetings five nights out of seven, so we were constantly in each other's company. Yet, we never talked about the topic that mattered to me the most: my boyfriend.

Every morning Papa left to work with the Bible workers he was assigned to while I stayed home alone all day. I watched TV, wrote to my friends and family, and read Harlequin romance books. Every time I finished reading a romance novel, I daydreamed that I was one of those fortunate women in love. When I returned from my dreams to reality, I cried and cried and cried. I couldn't talk to my friends because my father made sure I couldn't make long distance calls on the phone. The telephone was used for local calls only. Papa would return home around four o'clock. We had dinner together then attended the meetings.

Sometimes we went sightseeing. Other times we went grocery shopping. He introduced me to people who had children my age so that I would make friends and have a social life. I was not interested in meeting anybody. I wanted to be in Boston where I belonged.

During all this time, we never mentioned the reason why I was in California. He didn't broach the subject, and I didn't either. I wasn't sure how to address it, so I kept silent. Perhaps Papa wasn't sure how to approach it either. Otherwise, he would have said something sooner. I am just like my father—we don't leave things unsaid for a long time. When problems are not communicated, they fester, and sooner or later, they cause breakdowns in relationships. In fact, they cause explosive interactions among people.

One night we came back from the meetings and decided to have a late snack. As we were chatting, Papa made a comment that triggered an eruption of emotions. I proceeded to let him know that I was disappointed in him and resented him for treating me with disrespect. I went on and on and on. He never said a word. He just listened. Then I remember saying, "You are a dictator. If I don't do things your way, you punish me. And you do that to all your children. We don't want to talk to you. We don't want to have a relationship with you because you don't understand. You have no heart"

I didn't look at him while I was talking. If I looked at him I would have remembered that I was crossing the line and I would have had to stop. But after finished my last sentence, I looked at him and I knew. When I looked into his eyes, I knew that I had hurt him. He looked at me and said, "Someday you'll understand."

Suddenly, all the things I held against him—the intense negative feelings, the plans for revenge—vanished. My only concern was to remove the pain that I had just caused my father. I got up from my seat and went to him and sat on his lap. I apologized profusely. I felt an overwhelming sense of remorse and wished that I could take back everything I said. But I couldn't.

"Papa, you know that I love you. I really didn't mean what I said. I am just angry at you for the way you hurt me, and I wanted to hurt you the same way. You were just being my father. You did what you thought was best. Please forgive me. I love you."

He responded with a deep voice, "Je t'aime aussi ma chérie." (I love you too, my darling.)

I kissed his forehead then laid my head on his shoulder. We remained silent for a little while. Then suddenly he began to talk. He reminisced over our past and described our future: he was planning to bring the family together; he didn't like the separation that his education had imposed on all of us. He had high hopes and big dreams for me. He talked about my qualities and predicted that I would become a woman sought after in the world. I liked that.

He mentioned, "You have a great future ahead of you. I don't want you to make mistakes that will prevent you from getting there. You are young and there are many things that you don't understand yet. You have to trust your parents. I only want what's best for you. Since you were not willing to cooperate, I had to remove you from the situation. If you trust me, everything will work out fine. Trust me. Will you do that and work with me?"

"Yes," I committed.

"So the first thing we need to do is for us to get to know each other. Then we will learn to trust each other. I believe that you and I can develop a great relationship. I am your father after all." We talked for most of the night, finally going to bed at four o'clock in the morning. That night was one of the most definitive moments in our relationship

During that summer, Papa taught me many things. I learned a lot about relationships, especially with men. My father openly discussed with me any topic that I was interested in. In those days sex was a taboo topic; however, I was so comfortable with my dad that I could ask him any question and I knew he would tell me the truth. In most cases, it is the mother who speaks to her daughter about sex. In my case, it was my father who talked to me frankly and openly about sex. That was meaningful to me.

Time passed quickly and the summer was nearing an end. Papa confessed to me, "When I sent for you, I had no intention of sending you back to Boston. I was planning to take you back with me to Nebraska until the whole family reunited. But after we've spent this summer together, I can trust you to go back. If you promise me that you will not resume the relationship with that young man or any young men until you're eighteen, I will let you go back to Boston."

I hurriedly assured him that he could count on me. "I will not let you down, Papa. I promise."

The summer ended and my father put me on a plane back to Boston. I had a totally different attitude that day as I returned to Boston than I had on my way to Oakland. I left Boston with a resentful spirit, while upon my return, I had mixed feelings. Although I was anticipating going back home, I was also missing my dad. What seemed to be a curse just a few months earlier had turned out to be a blessing. I might have lost a boyfriend, but I gained a great friend, my papa. He gave me the greatest gift that summer. He gave me himself as a lifetime friend, confidant, and mentor.

The following two summers, Papa continued to work in Pastor Cleveland's evangelistic series. I asked to go with him, and he gladly accepted. My family reunited the following year, and I had to share Papa with everyone. But in the summers, I had him all to myself. I looked forward to those times together. They were precious times.

෴   ෴   ෴

It was my conversations with Papa that allowed me to develop communication skills with people. I debated a lot with Papa. I debated my way into and out of situations with him. Sometimes I won, and sometimes I lost. Actually, my father won most of the times. There were times when we debated on impersonal issues. One morning at family worship, we were studying about creation, the origin of God, etc. I shifted into my inquisitive mode and began to ask Papa myriads of questions. Since only Papa and I were involved in the discussion, he suggested that we resume our discussion after worship.

After worship Papa and I stayed in the living room to talk. I asked a lot of questions, "What if God didn't exist? Where did God come from? If God knows everything, why would He allow Adam and Eve to sin?"

My mother was livid. She was cooking breakfast and rushed to the room to tell my father not to allow me to continue with this train of questions. She said, "Naasson, that's enough! Don't let her talk about God that way. She is going too far! She has to stop."

Papa smiled and calmly said, "Leave her alone. It's better for me to know what she is thinking so I can help her. She will be all right. She is learning."

I appreciated the fact that Papa took time to listen to my foolishness and didn't call it foolish—he didn't condemn me. He was patient and gentle with me, and he seemed amused by some of the things I would say because he would laugh at them. Then he clarified them for me until I fully understood. That was exceptional.

৵৲   ৵৲   ৵৲

My relationships with men were sculpted by my relationship with Papa. He taught me how to relate to men. The ability to articulate myself under any circumstance was developed during our habitual conversations and debates. I was always attracted to intelligent men—men who articulated their thoughts well. Looks were not primary for me, but knowledge was definitely of primordial importance. Besides my sisters, I barely had any female friends. However, I had many male friends. Some were my boyfriends, others were platonic friends. I was fascinated by them.

I was nineteen years old when I accepted my first marriage proposal. My fiancé was a six-foot-three attractive young man who was planning to become an international lawyer. He was very intelligent and articulate. He was brilliant; I loved his brain. I had some of the most wonderful and fascinating conversations with him.

I admired men who could "turn a phrase." Later, I realized that I was attracted to him and other men with these qualities because of Papa's qualities. Naturally, I hadn't recognized this simple and yet profound fact earlier. My three-month engagement to my fiancé didn't materialize into marriage. I soon realized that my admiration for his genius was not strong enough to endure challenges in a marriage. I didn't love him. I loved Papa in him.

I remember when I met Baldwin in the cafeteria one Saturday afternoon. My two girlfriends and I sat at his table to eat lunch. I was instantly attracted to him; actually, the attraction was mutual. You could call it "love at first sight." He was tall, dark, and handsome. Not only did he possess an impressive stature, he had a silver tongue. He was very articulate and even regal. I looked into his eyes, and I saw them glitter as he smiled at me. I was captivated. As I was leaving the cafeteria, I declared to my friends, "He will be my husband."

Years later after Baldwin and I had severed our engagement, I rejected several proposals for exclusive relationships and marriage. My father didn't appreciate the fact that I was missing great opportunities from respectable and promising young men, and he vehemently expressed his feelings. One day, I decided to share with my father the reasons why I continuously rejected other men, seemingly waiting for Baldwin.

"Papa, Baldwin is the one I want. I love him for who he is— the good and the bad. The good characteristics outweigh the bad. You don't know him as well as I do. Do you want to know why I want Baldwin?"

"Yes, of course."

I proceeded to list and elaborate on the various qualities that I admired in Baldwin. First of all, he was intelligent and very articulate. I loved talking to him. There was no limit as to where our conversations could lead us. He knew so much about everything! (He is an avid reader, and to this day, when he reads, the world around him ceases to exist.)

Thirdly, we had the same cultural background. Although we didn't come from the same country and didn't speak the same language, there didn't seem to be any major cultural differences that existed between us. We came from families with similar values and practices. Our values and goals in life were so compatible! He was well trained by his parents. He was very refined and cultured.

We had no conflicts over who we were and where we wanted to be in life. Everything seemed to fit naturally. We were a good match.

Next, he was romantic. He loved to sing songs to me. He had the greatest voice in the world, I thought. I could listen to him all day long. (Now, I beg him not to sing.) He gave me flowers, cards, and gifts. He was attentive. He complimented and affirmed me all the time. He observed everything about me: the way I looked, my clothes, my hair, my physical characteristics.

Really, if a man wasn't like Baldwin or Papa, he didn't stand a chance. Papa was the one who nurtured my sisters and me. He observed us, making sure that we were dressed properly and complimenting us continuously. Baldwin was like Papa in that sense.

Our religious backgrounds were similar. I am a very religious person, and I wanted to marry a man who would be the spiritual leader of our home. Baldwin valued his relationship with God as much as I did. We prayed together every day. These prayers glued us together. I believe that the spiritual relationship we formed during our first two years together reunited us five years later and has kept our marriage on solid ground.

We also shared family values. Both of us believed that marriage was for keeps. Our parents were married for a long time. We wanted children and planned that I would stay home to raise them. I dated other men who didn't see the value of having an educated woman stay home to do the work that a babysitter or nanny could do. It was important to me that I would be the one to raise my children. Baldwin satisfied that desire.

The most important reason for choosing Baldwin was that I profoundly and genuinely loved him. We were madly in love with each other. I tried to purge myself of those feelings after we broke up, but it was no use. When Baldwin and I broke off our engagement two years after we met, I dated other eligible bachelors. A couple of them tried to erase Baldwin from my memory and cause me to fall in love with them, but none of them succeeded.

Papa listened intently as I explained to him why I was willing to pass opportunities to marry other men and wait for Baldwin. I met Baldwin when he was twenty years old. I was the first girl he had a serious relationship with. He was an idealist and needed to explore other options. I knew that he would come back to me. I was young; therefore, I would wait. I remember ending my monologue with, "Papa, I am convinced that God chose Baldwin for me. I will marry Baldwin. But if I don't, I will marry when he marries. Until then I will wait."

Papa paused for a moment, looking at me with admiration, he then said, "I am so proud of you. You know who you are and what you want; you will not settle for anything else. You are a woman of character. If you stay focused, you will have what you want. I applaud you and respect you for having these goals and dreams. I trust your judgment. You describe a great man in Baldwin. If God made the choice, you will marry Baldwin. Continue to trust in God to guide your life. You will have a great relationship when you marry. I will pray for you." We ended our conversation with Papa's prayer for Baldwin and me.

Papa never questioned my relationships with men again. Years later when Baldwin and I married and Papa knew him well, he told me, "You were right. He was worth waiting for. You made a great choice. He has all the qualities you described and more. Bravo, ma fille."

I was so happy that my father approved of my choice and confirmed it so positively. It meant a lot to me. After nearly 30 years of marriage, I still believe that Baldwin was God's choice for me.

After my wedding, Papa and I remained very close. He was my confidant during my years of adjustment to marriage. I looked to him for advice. Whenever I faced challenges with Baldwin, Papa would say, "Remember that you chose him." The extraordinary thing about my papa was that he never took sides or blamed Baldwin for anything. He never got emotional; he remained objective until the end. He didn't believe in divorce, so he worked with us, especially me, when Baldwin and I had reached an impasse.

There were times I looked to him for sympathy. He would listen to me and say, "I understand." Then he would encourage me to go back to my husband and work it out. To him, we were both his children for better or worse, until death did us part. His role was to encourage and empower us in our relationship. I was amazed at times at his sense of fairness and objectivity. I realize now that he was driven by integrity. I cannot imagine what my relationship with men would have been without Papa. I like who I've become, and I am thankful for the positive impact he had on my relationship with men and especially with Baldwin.

FOURTEEN

TILL DEATH DO
US PART

He saw her one Sabbath morning as she was entering church. He thought, "She is the prettiest little girl I know." Papa would later describe her to us with a twinkle in his eye. "She was beautiful! She was tiny with two long, shiny, black braids that went past her waist. She looked just like an Indian doll. I came closer to her and couldn't resist touching her braids. I thought to myself, 'Someday I will marry her.'" He married her ten years later.

This was my favorite story as a little girl. I enjoyed listening to it whenever Papa gave in to my insistent requests during the nights on our porch when he was home from work. It was fascinating to me that my father still stroked Maman's hair while he relayed the story to us. The passion he felt could be heard in his voice as he shared certain details about her with us. Each time he looked at her, it was as though he was seeing her for the first time. My favorite part of the story was the way he always ended it, "And she is still as beautiful today." My mother would giggle every time he reached this part.

I requested to hear that story over and over. I believe that my mother enjoyed hearing it as much as I did. I can imagine how affirmed she was by hearing this story. As my mother got satisfaction from listening to his memories, I, too, relished the warm and tender feelings that story evoked in me. I daydreamed about growing up to be as beautiful as my mom and marrying a man like my dad. After all, I looked the most like my mother. Every time my father recounted this story, I listened with impassioned curiosity as if hearing it for the first time.

Papa married Maman when he was twenty-four years old and Maman was seventeen. They remained married until the dawn of fifty years—forty-nine years, two months, and six days exactly—when they were parted by death. Maman grew up with Papa, matured with him, and went through her life cycles with him. She didn't know herself outside of their marriage. They struggled together, faced many challenges together, and raised nine children together.

Papa loved my mother and was devoted to her. He called her "Nao" or "Chérie"; she called him, "Chou"—all French terms of endearment for "Honey." Papa was affectionate with Maman yet cautious not to display too much. He brought her tokens from his trips, sometimes flowers. My mother loved to cuddle with him. He acknowledged her efforts, affirmed her beauty, teased her, and loved to make her laugh. The love that Papa expressed to Maman created an atmosphere where we, as children, felt loved and secure as well. They were a traditional couple: Papa worked outside of the home and provided for us in every way while Maman stayed home to raise us and governed the household affairs.

As leader of the home, Papa lay down the law and made the decisions for the family. However, when he was away, it was Maman who maintained the routine and consistency in the house by ensuring that his will was upheld at all times. As kids, sometimes we tried to seize the time Papa was away as an opportunity to do certain things we would otherwise not do in his presence. We would ask Maman for permission, and she would say, "You know your father would not approve of that," or "What would your father say?"

I would get so frustrated with her. She wouldn't let us get away with anything. Papa's presence was always felt, even in his absence. Sometimes I would ask her, "Maman, what do *you* say? What do you think? You always say what Papa wants. How about you, what do you want?"

She would respond, "Your father and I are one." I didn't understand it then. I used to think that she had no thoughts of her own because she mirrored him so often. It seemed that she was dependent on him to make all decisions in the house. I wanted her to stand up to him and argue her views and do as she pleased, but she never did. My father was the leader of our home, and my mother enabled him.

I realize that who I have become is partly a reaction to who my mother was. My mother is soft in nature and does not speak too loud. I had vowed never to be like her because I perceived her as weak and a push-over, catering to every whim and fancy of my father. I admired Papa and wanted to be like him instead. He was strong, assertive, intelligent, and powerful. Along the way, I fashioned myself after him.

Then I got married. I was like my father and unlike my mother. I had a mind of my own; I was educated and determined to express my thoughts and feelings without reservation. Baldwin and I were both miserable. I couldn't get Baldwin to react the way I wanted him to. Before we got married, he was attentive, affectionate, and expressive. Afterwards, he forgot special dates, was reserved, and only communicated when it was necessary. I was unhappy. I tried to figure out the source of the problem. I concluded that, of course, it was Baldwin.

Then, I began to observe that whenever Papa, my brothers, my brother-in-law, and even Baldwin were around my mother they were different. They would do anything for her. She could ask for anything, and they would jump. I wondered why. It reached the point where I would have Maman ask Baldwin to do certain things for me. Her wish was his command.

I decided to approach Papa concerning my observation and perception of his relationship with Maman. I said to him, "Papa, I never heard what Maman wanted; it was always what you wanted. She didn't have a voice. I didn't feel that you made room for her to express views that contradicted yours. She never disagreed with you. She had the right to disagree with you, but I felt that you didn't allow her to. You ruled and Maman obeyed. I think that was wrong, and I vowed not to act like her. Today, I am miserable in my marriage because of you. You caused me to be this way. I was determined to be different. "

Papa listened with a smile on his face, and then he responded, "So you thought that I was the ruler. That was not and is not the case. Just because you don't hear your mother doesn't mean that she does not have a voice. She knows how to get me to do anything. She lets me take the lead, but she leads in her own way. She can defend herself and express her views clearly and vehemently. Most of the times, I executed her wishes, and still do. But you didn't know that. She would not disagree with me in front of her children or anyone else. But she also ruled."

I was shocked. Then Papa said something that was a profound lesson for me. "The secret is that your mother knew how to speak to me and when to speak to me. I would do anything for her because of the way she spoke to me. She preserved my dignity and elevated me in front of you and everybody else."

That blew me away. I responded, "Papa that is wonderful! But it would have been helpful if you had shared this very important part with us. It would have impacted all of us."

I began to watch Maman closely. I talked to her and discovered that we shared similar views and traits in many areas. Even though I am the picture image of her, I had become more like my father. After my talk with Papa, I began to channel my personality into the submissive manners of my mother to benefit my marriage. I have learned and am still learning valuable lessons by looking at her through my father's eyes instead of my own. She is a wise lady. I admire her so much more today.

ॐ   ॐ   ॐ

Maman valued her husband. She appreciated his efforts to make her happy. She would say, "God gave me a good husband." In return, she was always supportive of his dreams, career, projects, and decisions. She seemed to allow him to do whatever he was committed to. She admired him, was in love with him, and beamed when he walked in the room. She saw him through his strengths, not his weaknesses.

I remember how Papa enjoyed his daily homecoming from work. Maman would dress nicely, look attractive, and smell good as though she was going on a date or expecting a special guest for dinner. She was always ready for his arrival. If he came home late after our suppertime, she would not eat until he did. Although the table was set for the family at suppertime, Papa's setting was special. His portion of the table would be set for a king: china, silverware, and crystal were used for every meal. She served him. He continuously complimented her on her cooking.

I would hear him say, "Nao, thank you for the food. It was good!" or "My compliments to the chef." One of his comments always amused me: "That was delicious. I must admit that it needed more salt. But it was still delicious."

I thought that my mother spoiled my father too much. She treated him like a king. She even gave him foot massages. She epitomized Romans 12:10, which says, "Honor one another above yourselves" (NIV). At times when we protested over the fact that she treated him better than us, Maman would say, "When all of you are gone, he is the one who will be left with me. So I'm going to take good care of him so that he can live a long life."

Papa was amused by those discussions and concluded that we were just jealous, but he enjoyed Maman's treatment. Papa used to tell me, "I am who I am today because of your mother. She is a good woman."

 ᑦᔕ   ᑦᔕ   ᑦᔕ

Papa worried that Maman sacrificed a lot as a pastor's wife. They lived a nomadic life—Maman was frequently a single parent, neglected while Papa traveled, and she put some of her dreams aside for Papa to reach his. She did not complete college, and although she wanted to develop a catering company, Papa came first.

I felt that Maman sacrificed too much as a pastor's wife, and I vowed never to marry a pastor. In fact, all of my six sisters and I swore that we would never marry pastors. When I was in college, I avoided all the young men who majored in theology. I didn't want to even get acquainted with them for fear that I might like one of them. I thought that I was safe with Baldwin, who majored in chemistry and psychology. I didn't know then that he was running away from God's "calling."

Seven years after we got married, I found out when he "surrendered" to the calling. He chose to break the news to me when we were visiting my parents for Christmas. I felt trapped. I was angry. I did not want to be a pastor's wife. I said, "Why me Lord?" My sisters were disappointed with Baldwin. They felt so sorry for me. They thought that I was deceived and that was a justifiable cause for a divorce. So far, I am the only daughter who is married to a pastor.

When I shared the news with Papa, naturally, he was elated. We talked for a long time. He told me many things, but the one that I remembered was, "If God really called your husband, I suggest that you don't get in his way. If you do, God can move you out of His way." That did it. I was motivated by fear.

I told Baldwin that as long as he could balance his responsibilities of pastor, parent, and husband, and as long as my children and I could continue to live according to our understanding of Christian principles and not according to the dictates of church members, then I would support him in pastoral ministry. He agreed and has kept his promise. In retrospect, I am glad that I didn't stand in his way. I have remained true to my authentic self, never presenting myself on false pretenses to church members. It's been effective for me and I truly enjoy sharing Baldwin's ministry. I have become an integral part of his work; I feel now that God willed me to be an agent of transformation with my husband.

The last words I spoke to Papa at his death bed were, "Papa, don't worry that your ministry will end with you. Baldwin and I will continue what you began." Currently, Baldwin and I are the only members of my family who work for the church. Papa dedicated his whole life to working for God and the church. I will not let it end with him. Today, I walk in the footsteps of my father. I am amazed to see how far God can lead us if we allow Him.

☙   ☙   ☙

As I observed my parents through the years, I learned that besides commitment the most important ingredient of a happy marriage is acceptance—accepting the other unconditionally. It was difficult to do at first, but I had to learn to fully accept my husband as he was if we were going to be happy and fulfilled in our relationship. It took years, but once I learned and accepted that principle, my relationship was transformed.

At the early stages of our marriage, I was on an emotional roller coaster. During my years of adjustment in my marriage, I looked to Papa for advice; he was my confidant. When I shared my problems about Baldwin with Papa, he didn't take sides. I marveled at his sense of objectivity. He hid his own emotions and remained impartial through the end. I was his daughter and Baldwin was his son. His advice was always intended to benefit our marriage. For him, divorce was not an option. At times he would remind me, "You made your choice. The commitment you made was 'til death do you part', so you have to work it out." I eventually realized that it was my commitment to my marriage and our acceptance of each other that made a difference. We are happily committed to each other "until death do us part."

My parents expressed commitment to each other under numerous circumstances, even in sickness and in health. Papa was losing his sight and the doctors had tried everything except surgery. Finally, the ophthalmologist told him that he would do a surgical procedure that would surely address the problem. The ophthalmologist was very enthusiastic and hopeful. He told Papa that the procedure would not be very long and when he came out of it, he would regain his vision. Every member of the family was hopeful and prayed that God would take care of the problem and restore Papa's sight. On the day of the surgery, Papa prayed, "May God's will be done."

When Papa returned to the doctor's office for the unveiling, the doctor was cheerful and very optimistic. When he removed the gauze from Papa's eyes, he asked triumphantly, "What do you see?" Papa responded that he could only see shapes and forms but could not clearly distinguish facial features. Disappointment was very apparent in the doctor's face and his reaction.

He said, "But I did everything right, you should see me clearly right now." He examined Papa's eyes. "But everything looks all right. I don't understand why it didn't work. I am confused. Your vision should have improved tremendously."

With a resigned voice, Papa offered words of consolation, "You have done your best. I thank you very much for your efforts."

He sadly looked at Papa and stated, "I'm so sorry; it should have worked. I don't know why it didn't work. I'm so sorry." He left the room confused.

Papa and Maman left for home, never to see the doctor again. When they reached home, Maman said to Papa, "I am going to pray that God restores your vision."

Papa quickly responded, "Nao, please don't do that. I don't want you to pray for me. If God wanted me to see, He would have allowed me to see. Whatever happens to my sight is well with me. May His name be praised. My life is in His hands."

As time passed, Papa's sight disintegrated. He recognized our shapes and silhouettes. Then he could only see light, which dimmed slowly. Then, finally, he saw nothing.

One day he called Maman and said, "I need to speak to you." From the tone of his voice, Maman assumed that it was important. Papa said to Maman, "Cherie, I cannot see any more. I am going to rely completely on you. Your eyes will be my eyes. You will read for me, see for me, and translate the world to me. I love you, and I trust you implicitly with my life. Nao, my life is in your hands."

Maman smiled and said, "Jusqu'a la mort (until death do us part). You don't ever have to worry about anything; you are in good hands. "

Actually, he had always been in good hands. When Papa became blind, Maman continued to care for him. She still allowed him to have the final word, even in finances. She could have done anything she wanted without his knowledge or consent, but she always consulted him. When I commented on that, she said, "He is very fragile right now. He is vulnerable; he cannot see. I have to make sure that he knows that his blindness has not changed anything in our relationship." Then she smiled and said, "He is still the boss."

At the sunset years of their lives together, Papa frequently praised Maman for being a wonderful wife. He told her that God had created her just for him, and he hoped that she had experienced joy and satisfaction with him as he had with her. She assures me that she did. She remained his committed companion, catering and caring for him tenderly until death parted them.

FIFTEEN

BEING CONNECTED

Integrity is the alignment of one's beliefs, convictions, and commitments with their actions. It has to do with living life with a destined resolve. Everything in Papa's life pointed to serving and glorifying God. He performed every task with unflinching integrity. People who live in accordance with God's will are connected to Him. This connection creates a being unrecognizable to others. One might say that such a person is extraordinary because he lives an extraordinary life and does extraordinary things. He then becomes an instrument through which God operates. God and he become of the same mind. They become one.

Such people are awesome. Nothing is unattainable because they know that the mighty God in them empowers them to do anything. They are bold, focused, and committed. They take risks, stepping out in faith, because they are fearless, unabashed, and daring. They are confident because they believe that they are heirs, they trust in God, and they have peace. In essence, to be this powerful one needs to be and stay connected with God.

I knew that my father was a powerful man ever since I was a youngster in Haiti. His influence and work marveled men. As far as my memory serves me, I knew that people revered Papa. Years after his death when people speak of him, they speak with reverence, admiration, and respect. Disciples always surrounded him. They treated him as though he was God Jr. I suppose, since he considered himself to be God's son, Papa was His mouthpiece and His hands. People around me believed it too. They had good reason to believe; they had enough evidence.

People were healed from incurable diseases because Papa prayed for and anointed them. People were raised from their deathbeds because Papa called on the name of God. Evil spirits were cast out because Papa authorized them to come out in the name of Jesus. He was awesome.

I frequently meet people from New York, Massachusetts, and Illinois who, when they find out whose daughter I am, anxiously tell me about their experience with Papa. This was the case with a lady I recently met in New York who shared her experience with me. She recounted that years ago her husband had been diagnosed with epilepsy and suffered terrible seizures. As time progressed, the seizures became more and more frequent. It reached a point where the seizures were occurring weekly. Sometimes she would receive phone calls regarding her husband falling into a seizure on the train, in the street, and other places. She didn't know what to do.

One day while at church, she went to my father, who was her pastor. She told him that she was tired of the situation. She was at her wit's end and didn't know where to turn. She truly loved her husband but wasn't sure how long she could endure the situation.

Papa told her, "Hold on, I am coming to visit you and your husband at home." He talked with them about their relationship and the state of their relationship with God. Following the conversation, he said, "Let's pray." Papa prayed for the family, and when he spoke to God about the husband, he laid his hands on him and prayed for his healing. When Papa got up from his knees, he looked at the man and said, "You are healed."

One month passed after Papa's visit, then two months, then one year, and then two years. Nineteen years later, the man still had not had one seizure. Her husband is still alive and healthy. She is eternally grateful.

There was one incident I remember from when I was very young, maybe about ten years old. I remember it clearly. In those days, people were baptized in the river. That Saturday afternoon the church had gathered by the riverbank to sing as the people were dipped into the water and ushered to the sheds to change. I was standing with my brothers and sisters close to Maman. Papa extended his hand to help this man into the water, and as he started to speak, the man started to mumble some undistinguished words. My father continued to speak, as though unaware of the distraction. As Papa said "I now baptize you in the name of the Father," the man started to scream.

"No, No, No. You will not have him. He's mine," the man shouted.

Papa continued to say, "In the name of the Son, and in the name of the Holy Ghost." By then you could hardly hear him because it sounded like numerous voices talking and screaming and threatening at the same time. As Papa bent to immerse the man in the water, the man started to fight with him. He would not let Papa take him down.

My father must have realized that he was dealing with a man possessed with evil spirits. Papa attempted many times to take him down, but the resistance was strong. Meanwhile, the church members had stopped singing. They were watching the event evolving before them with fear. I was terrified. I remember hanging onto somebody's hand or skirt for dear life.

Papa noticed that the people were not singing, he commanded them to sing. As he was struggling to baptize this man, he called on the elders and deacons to pray. Papa never removed his eyes from the man. The struggle continued for a while. He held the man and pressed him down, but the man was strong enough to get back up. They went up and down, up and down many times. The man and his voices were screaming all sorts of things. He said things like, "We're a legion. He's one of us, and we're not going to lose him to you or your God. We will kill him first."

My father held him, pressed him down with all his might, and ordered, "In the name of Jesus, get out of this man." With that, he took him all the way down under the water. I could see him struggle as he was taking him down. The man was finally baptized.

The people started singing louder and shouting, "Thank you Lord! Hallelujah!" But when Papa raised the man from the water, he was unconscious. My father handed him over to the deacons to carry him away. They checked him and told Papa that he was not breathing—he was dead. Without hesitation, Papa told the deacons to lay him down and leave him alone. He continued with the baptism as though the incident hadn't happened. Imagine the mixed feelings that people were experiencing that moment.

I was stupefied. I wondered why my father didn't attend to this dead man before he continued with the baptisms. In fact, I was sure that he was going to postpone the baptisms, but he continued until he finished with the last person.

Then he marched on to the dead body. Everybody followed him. He turned around and asked the people to stay where they were and pray. He knelt to the ground where the man laid and said, "My brother, wake up; you are now free in Jesus Christ." The man woke up and stood to his feet. My father prayed for him and for the other newly baptized members. Then, they all went to change.

The bystanders were amazed. Some were whispering to each other. Others were jumping up and down, praising God. I heard a man say, "My God! What kind of man is this?"

I was in shock. He never mentioned a word about the incident when we went home, and I was too scared to speak.

People talked about that event for months. In spite of all the great things people said about Papa, he never boasted about anything he did. Instead, he always gave God the glory and credit. One of his favorite responses was, "Glory to God." That's how Papa was. He was focused. He didn't stop to talk to anyone before or after an incident. Sometimes, when he was on a mission from God, he seemed to be in a trance. He would not speak to anyone. He would not allow himself to get distracted by anyone. He was a powerful man of God because he stayed humble and connected.

In spite of the reverence that was given to him, his children were never allowed to be proud or arrogant. We felt privileged to be his children, but we never felt special or superior as many expected. In fact, when the supernatural occurred, we were more fearful than anything else. Papa did his best to keep us away from the crowd or events. With people, he was the man of God; with us, he was just Papa.

Another gift that Papa possessed was a revelation of his future. He seemed to know about any big event that would occur in his life ahead of time. Years before Papa lost his sight he knew that it was going to happen. Yet, we never noticed a moment of fret on his part.

Twenty five years prior to that fateful turn, my cousin Danielle took a speech class. Her class project was to prepare and present a speech to the class. She approached Papa for help. Knowing that he was a great speaker, she asked him about his sermon/ speech-writing techniques. Papa gave her some ideas and confessed that the way he wrote his sermon required him to do a lot of memorization. He included a lot of passages and verses so that he would be forced to memorize them. He said, "I prepare my sermons this way because I need to memorize the Bible. I will need to rely on memorization because I will become blind someday."

As Papa was losing his sight, he never complained, never showed sadness. He was always courageous. No wonder! He knew that it was going to happen. We were concerned as to the impact of his blindness on him. We were sad for him and didn't know what to do for him. We were more worried about his blindness than he was. Whenever we would question him about God's silence in the situation, he always responded, "I don't question the things that happen in my life. If God chooses to allow it to happen, who am I to question? Que la volonte de Dieu soit faite." (May God's will be done.)

His attitude eased the pain we all were experiencing and made it bearable for us all. I was always amazed at his attitude. We weren't aware of his foreknowledge of his blindness. We should have figured it out, given that he was rarely surprised about events in his and our lives. I wish that he had told me about it. We could have shared the pain of anticipation with him. It must have been hard to accept. But knowing my father, he always tried to spare us of undue duress, especially when it came to my mother. He suffered alone in order to spare us. I am sure he did.

Papa was connected to God. He was able to do all these things and more because of his connection. When we were in Haiti, he used to go to the mountains for days to meditate, fast, and pray. He said that he needed time to reflect in silence and seek the face of God. Sometimes he went for one day, like on Sunday. He would do that at least once a month. Whenever he said, "Nao, Je reviens, Je vais a la montagne," (Nao, I will be back, I am going to the mountain) we knew what the purpose was for his trip.

Time alone with God was a vital element of his power. Meditation was the focus: allowing one's mind to go blank for a while so that God may enter in and communicate with you. That was the source of his power. That's where he received power from God. He said that that's how he connected with God. Sometimes he would go with his prayer partner, but most of the time, he went alone. It was his continuous "burning bush" experience, I guess. When he returned, he could do anything. Nothing could shake him. He was focused, connected, and powerful. He was solidly grounded.

When we moved to the U.S. and Canada, he said that he had to be more intentional to stay focused. "It is too distracting," he used to say. When in the U.S., he was going to school full time, he was working full time, and he was a father full time. Of course, being a full-time father was foreign to him. But if you ask any of my siblings about the best time in their childhood as a family, they will say it was when we lived in Lincoln, Nebraska—and I agree. Although this was a memorable time for us, it was difficult for Papa to stay focused. He had to create his mountain experience at the park for the day.

In Canada though, he was able to steal away for spiritual renewal more frequently than when we lived in the U.S. He was powerful there as well. His reputation preceded him there. People came for all kinds of reasons. God worked through him in a mighty way.

Papa was known as a man of prayer. He mastered that gift. I depended on his prayers as much as church members and non-members did. People came from everywhere to have him pray for them. I could write volumes about the miracles that occurred through his ministry.

After his first retirement, he moved back to Canada from New York, bought thirty-one acres of land with a big house on it and a number of streams. He wanted it to be the family vacation house, but mostly he wanted to build a house of prayer for people to come to. He felt that people needed time away from the busyness of life to renew in the Lord. As people heard of it, they came. Some came for a week or a weekend. Papa had a prayer formula that people followed. It had to be followed for either seven days or three days. Miracles resulted out of using this formula.

When he lost his sight and moved to Florida, he insisted on having another house of prayer because people were following him there. He seemed to have even more power while being blind. I suppose it's because he could concentrate more on God. Since he couldn't move around that much, he felt that people could come to him and he would pray with and for them. My mother didn't think that it was a good idea. They were retired, but they couldn't rest. People came uninvited, because Papa's home was a house of prayer.

Finally, he wrote a book about this miracle formula. My sister Jasmine convinced him to write this book to memorialize his ministry of prayer and empower people to use the formula on their own. The book could impact more people than he could impact in person. So he conceded. He dictated and we wrote. My mother and my sisters wrote by hand and Jasmine, who could type more than one hundred words per minute, typed the book.

The end product was called *Sept Jours Avec Dieu*—in English it is called *Seven Days With God*. People bought the book like hot potatoes. We received phone calls all the time from people telling us about the results of their week of prayer. It worked. I am so glad that he was alive to hear so many of the miracles that took place through that book.

Every time I attend an event in a Haitian community, someone shares a miracle that God performed in their life through my father's prayers. Once in a while, someone calls us to share their miracle out of using his formula. A gentleman from Senegal, Africa, told me that someone gave him a copy of the book and it impacted his prayer life and others. I am glad that Papa left a legacy behind.

Jesus said in Mark 11:22-24, "Have faith in God. . . . I tell you the truth, if anyone says to this mountain, 'Go, throw yourself into the sea,' and does not doubt in his heart but believes that what he says will happen, it will be done for him. Therefore, I tell you, whatever you ask for in prayer, believe that you have received it, and it will be yours" (NIV). Papa truly believed these verses and lived them literally.

These are but a few of the numerous miracles that God performed through my father. He was truly connected to God. We never boasted about being his children. People were always amazed to find us so humble. They somehow expected us to be haughty and proud, even stuck up. A friend of my sister Eve said to us, "You guys don't really take advantage of who you are. If only you knew! People think the world of your father. If you wanted to, people would eat out of your hands, just because you are Pastor Prosper's children."

We were never raised to be that way. Papa always said that it was God in him who did those things. We didn't do anything. We considered ourselves servants of the people just as Papa considered himself to be. But I am happy and privileged to have been his daughter because of the example he gave me. My utmost goal is to be as connected, as powerful, and as committed to integrity as he was.

SIXTEEN

THERE MUST BE A REASON

Shortly after graduating with my doctoral degree, Papa's health worsened. His blood pressure and glucose were skyrocketing. He was taken to the hospital several times by ambulance. The family became increasingly concerned. He underwent numerous tests, but the diagnoses were always inconclusive. Doctors were speculating, but they gave us no specific indication about what was happening with Papa. Finally, a doctor decided to do an MRI, and the results indicated that Papa had a terminal condition—a malignant brain tumor—with a life expectancy of three months. Since the tumor had already reached a level four of severity when he was diagnosed, the physician felt that it would be futile to attempt surgery.

I watched my dad go from a wholesome person to an invalid over the next eight months. We helped him walk, dress, and take his medicine. His blood pressure and diabetes worsened and caused debilitating digestive issues. It reached the point where he could no longer care for his basic needs: feeding, bathing, going to the bathroom. Brushing his teeth was the only thing he was able to do by himself.

He enjoyed listening to the music though. One thing we knew for sure was that Papa enjoyed music. He had a favorite inspirational religious singer, T. Marshall Kelly. Whenever we played Kelly's CD, Papa hummed along. So, I brought more of his favorite artist, and we played him Kelly's CDs over and over and over.

I can understand why he liked Kelly because his voice evokes a sense of peace, serenity, and wholeness. He also had a history with T. Marshall Kelly. They worked together with Evangelist E. E. Cleveland one summer in Detroit, Michigan. Kelly was the official singer for that crusade, and Papa truly enjoyed his music ministry every night. He would sometimes exclaim, "Now this is a man of God!" So it was fitting that he would spend his last days on earth listening to an inspiring "man of God."

Then his memory started to regress. I noticed that his memory was waning, so I decided to talk to him and retrieve as much information from him as I could to document for future generations. I asked him questions about his childhood, his ministry, our family, our roots, and anything else I could think of. I was amazed at how he remembered some details so well at that time. I noticed that the memories of his childhood and youth were more vivid than those of his adult life, especially those leading to the time before his sickness. It's as though he was gradually reverting to childhood.

As Papa began to lose his memory, details of his life began to dissipate. He began to forget colleagues and church members, then his relatives, his children, his wife, and lastly, his only brother. There were moments of awareness, but after a while, he just didn't communicate. His speech progressively became incoherent. Finally, he didn't speak at all.

Sometimes I sat in the room just watching him either lying on his bed or sitting quietly in his chair. I thought about all the times we'd shared and memories we'd made together. It was inconceivable that my father had deteriorated so much in such a short period of time. There was nothing that I could do. I was sad; I felt so helpless!

As his illness progressed, the family decided not to allow visitors in the house. We didn't want people to see him in his condition. Furthermore, he was not speaking to anyone at that time, and we were not sure that he would recognize them. We wanted people to always remember our father as the dynamic, powerful, and extraordinary man of God they knew. After all, he was a prince among his people. Numerous people who wanted to see him felt cheated by our decision. They felt that it was unfair of us not to allow them to say good-bye to their pastor, mentor, and friend. In spite of their insistence, we were not moved by their concerns. We wanted Papa to die with dignity.

Although we felt strongly about keeping Papa away from the public, there were some people who forced themselves into his private chambers. They didn't call; they just came to the house and insisted on seeing him. Two such persons were Jean-Hubert and his friend. Jean-Hubert considered himself to be Papa's son; he felt entitled. It was Jean-Hubert and his friend who volunteered to drive my parents' car from New York to Florida when Papa retired. Jean-Hubert reminded us how he became very close to Papa and the family as he followed him around, learning so much from him. He insisted on seeing Papa, and we finally conceded.

Jean-Hubert spent his visit having a monologue with Papa. He talked for quite a while with no response from Papa. When he was ready to leave he said to Papa, "Père (Father—as he always called him), I want my blessing. I am not leaving before you bless me. You have to pray for me, Père. Pray for me."

I will never forget what happened next. Without hesitation, my father attempted to stand, and Jean-Hubert helped him up. To our amazement, Papa began to pray. He was speaking audibly, which he hadn't done in several weeks! He talked to God about specific situations in Jean-Hubert's life and blessed him. I am not sure that he recognized Jean-Hubert because he didn't speak to him directly and never mentioned his name in the prayer. He referred to Jean-Hubert as "this young man."

In the prayer, Papa predicted that Jean-Hubert was going to experience serious challenges in his life that would shake his faith and discourage him. Papa prayed that God would give him all the strength he needed to go through the trials that were looming. He encouraged Jean-Hubert to hold strong and not give up because God would be with him through the storm, and if he had faith, he would be victorious. Papa concluded with, "Be not afraid or terrified. For the Lord your God will be with you. He will never leave you nor forsake you."

My mother, siblings, and I were dumbfounded. Papa had prayed powerfully. Jean-Hubert was elated that Papa had blessed him. As Jean-Hubert was leaving, he turned to Papa and declared, "Père, you still got the power." Following Jean-Hubert's departure, Papa reversed to his previous state. I could not understand how Papa, who had not talked for weeks, suddenly stood up to pray upon request. He had not spoken to anyone, not even Maman, yet he had been used powerfully to prepare Jean-Hubert for the struggles he said he passed through after Papa died.

Later, we realized that the mere mention of God's name would stimulate some response from Papa. It was as though he was in a coma and came out of it every time he heard the name of God uttered; then, just as suddenly, he'd reverse to the coma. He came alive and spoke only on matters of God, nothing else. We all knew that it had to do with Papa and his relationship with God. His life was so consumed by God that the last vestiges of his brain remained true to Him. Since he knew that he was going to die, we concluded that he must have decided to remove himself from earthly matters to dwell in the heavenly realm awaiting his last breath.

Still, I was constantly baffled to see Papa come alive when he heard the Bible read or a familiar religious song. One day, my baby sister Tantie sat across from his bed with a Bible and asked him, "Papa, do you want me to read the Bible for you?" He nodded, so Tantie began reading. She started with a psalm. As she was reading, Papa joined in and recited the psalm along with her. I was surprised. When Tantie completed the first psalm, I asked her to read another one and then another. It was fascinating to hear him recite each of them when he had not spoken to anyone for a while. We'd begun to think that he couldn't speak anymore. I decided to test him by asking Tantie to read a chapter from the book of John. As she began reading it, he joined in and recited the whole passage. From that point forward, I continued to read for him during my visits, and he never once failed to recite along with my reading.

ৎৎ৽   ৎৎ৽   ৎৎ৽

I struggled with the reality of Papa's illness and began to question God, "How could a man who was so connected to You, who lived as Your mouthpiece, who performed great miracles in peoples' lives on Your behalf end up this way? How could this happen? Where are You? How could You allow Your devoted and relentless servant to devolve to this level? Is this how You repay him for a lifetime of service and sacrifice? Why him? Why not somebody else who really deserves it?"

I couldn't understand why God would allow this to happen to my father. I grappled with these questions. Papa's only purpose for living was to please God. What did Papa do to deserve this kind of treatment from God? Since Papa believed that there was a lesson to be learned in every situation, I thought, "Surely, there must be a lesson to be learned from this." I searched and searched, but nothing seemed to make sense.

Truly, I couldn't believe that this was right, that a man of God could die like this. I thought it was unfair. I decided that God should change His mind and heal my father; I prayed for it every day. When healing no longer seemed plausible, I convinced my-self that it was a set up for Papa's greatest testimony: God was planning Papa's return from death. When we were sure that he was gone, the heartache of losing my dad was compounded by feelings of abandonment by God.

Then I stopped to think, "Who am I to decide how God ended my father's life?" The fact is that Papa would have repeated the very same thing he had always said whenever I questioned God's directives in his life. He would have told me, "Ma fille, I do not question how God chooses for my life to turn out. My life is in His hands; I accept whatever He chooses to do with me." When I re-butted with alternatives, he would give me his typical response, "We will not continue with this conversation. God has spoken. C'est fini."

I thought of the biblical story of Job. A man righteous in the sight of God found himself in a predicament that he could not un-derstand. He lost all of his possessions, his children had died, and he became a leper. Others ridiculed him, saying, "Surely, this man has sinned and is paying for his sins." Although he was a servant of God, he was abandoned by his friends because of his situation. Finally, like me, he began to question God.

I took God's response in Job personally. God asks, "Who is this that darkens my counsel with words without knowledge? . . . Where were you when I laid the earth's foundation? . . . Have you ever given orders to the morning or shown the dawn its place. . . . Does rain have a father? . . . Can you set up God's dominion over the earth?... Who endowed the heart with wisdom or gave under-standing to the mind?" (Job 38:2-36, NIV). God continues, "Will the one who contends with the Almighty correct him? (40:2) Who has a claim against me that I must pay? Everything under heaven belongs to me" (41:11).

Then, like Job in chapter 42, I had to respond "I know that you can do all things; no plan of yours can be thwarted. . . . Surely

I spoke of things I did not understand, things too wonderful for me to know" (Job 42:2, 3).

All I wanted was for my papa to remain the prince that he was known to be by others and die with dignity. But who am I to question God? I decided to believe, as Papa did, that our lives are in God's hands; we must accept whatever He chooses to do with us.

After Papa's death, I came to the conclusion that my father was a human being who was susceptible to all the ills of this earth. He was as vulnerable as anyone else. We had elevated him to a superhuman level, but he was a man just like all of us. The difference is that Papa caused his life to matter by surrendering it to the will of God. He was convinced and committed to live out his purpose on earth: to love and serve God and humankind. He fought a good fight. He lived life to its fullest extent. The end of his life did not determine its quality. I can confidently say that my father walked with God all his life. And that's all that matters.

After all the years of questioning God through debates with Papa, I had finally found the reason. There was a lesson to be learned from Papa's illness and death—the greatest lesson he'd tried to teach me throughout our life together—it is not for me to question God's actions; it is my job to accept them. That's all.

AFTERWORD

TRIBUTE TO PAPA

I paid tribute to my father at his funeral. Although it was one of the most difficult things I've had to do, I wanted to honor him and share with others who Naasson M. B. Prosper was to me. Following is the speech I presented:

Last summer (1998), almost a year ago, my father came to visit me for my doctoral graduation. We spent a week together, going for long walks and conversing amidst each morning's dew. One morning he calmly stated, "I can die now because I know that all my children will be successful in life and you will support each other. It pleases me to see that my children are so close to each other." He began to reflect on his life and give me counsel on his approaching death.

"Papa," I said, "If you die before me, I will honor you by paying tribute to you at your funeral."

For a moment, he paused and questioned, "Tu crois que tu peux faire ca?" (Are you sure that you are tough enough to do that?) Then he added quickly, "Tu es une grande dame. Tu peux faire tout ce que tu veux. " (You are a great lady. You can do anything you set your mind to do.)

That's my papa. That's who he was for me, one who always believed in me. My father caused me to be who I am today. He provided me an open-minded and supportive environment to communicate in. The way he listened was rare. Nothing was unattainable in the span of his confidence in me. He frequently said to me, "Tu es une femme de grand courage, avec de rare qualites. Tu accompliras de grands exploits dans ta vie" (You are a woman of great strength, a woman of rare qualities. You will accomplish great things in life.)

On one of those memorable walks, he suggested, "I guess I didn't do such a bad job as your father; look what you've become." That statement was one of the best compliments that I ever received from my father. It shows that he was more than satisfied as a result of his parenting; he was proud of me. I was proud to be his daughter. We were both fulfilled and gushed with joy and love for each other. We were profoundly connected.

I am so grateful that I shared with Papa what I intended to say at his funeral. Truthfully, I don't recall all that I said. But it doesn't matter, because he heard it all. When I finished he stopped, speechless for a moment. Then he burst out saying, "Gloire a Dieu! Je n'ai pas vecu en vain. " (Praise God! I have not lived in vain.)

I am so glad that I gave him those flowers when he was alive. I stand here as a "Grande dame" to pay tribute to my father. I stand here to celebrate with you the great life of a great man, Pastor Naasson Belizaire Prosper, my father.

I say pastor because that was part of his name. It became his identity. Even though there were times when I would not embrace his devotion to the church, I admired his undauntable stand for it. He defined what and who a pastor is and should be. If you wanted to understand what a pastor was like, you just had to spend time with him and you would certainly know.

My father was the greatest prophet I know. He personified the very qualities that I admire in the prophets of the Bible. He was a man of integrity with strong character and a bold, unfaltering faith. A man of deep devotion, he was an extraordinary transformational speaker for God's use.

Papa was renowned for his life of consistent prayer. When the doctor told him that a biopsy should be done in order to ascertain the extent of his illness, Papa responded, "Let me consult God. I will get back with you as soon as He tells me what to do."

I was in shock! If it were me, I would have been too eager to say yes. I would have talked to God later. But not Papa. All he could think of was consulting his God. Such was his life under all circumstances. He consulted God for every action he performed. God was the center of his life. I admire and respect that.

I confess that I relied heavily on him to consult with God on my behalf when I needed to make a major decision in my life. One time when I was facing serious challenges in my life he encouraged me by saying, "God is preparing you for the great work He wants you to do. So go through it with courage. Hold your head up high. When you come out of it, you will be strong. You will shine. Only then you will be ready to make a difference."

Papa was preparing me for the life of ministry and the ministry of life. He helped me to embrace the teachings of life to better serve others. He saw me through the eyes of love and greatness. With this kind of support, I was destined to succeed. And I never wanted to disappoint him.

Three themes saturated Papa's life: fervent devotion to God; unshakeable commitment to his family; and an undeniable stand for people. Papa was a passionate expression of all three and lived life to fulfill them. Papa accomplished so much in his lifetime: he was a warrior, a champion of the human cause, and an extraordinary, transformational speaker. Il etait l'homme de Dieu et l'homme du people. (He was a man of God and a man of his people.) He was a leader who created new possibilities for his family, his church, and his people. There were no boundaries to what he would do for them. He lived to make a difference in every life he touched. He gave so much too so many people. He extended himself through unabashed generosity. Papa was a son and servant of God, a loving and devoted father, and a minister par excellence.

There is no doubt that he will be missed. Permit me to tell you what we, his family, will miss. We will miss his bass voice when we sang together, his words of encouragement and admonition, his sweet kisses and strong embraces, his jokes and hefty laughter, his prayers, his blessings on each of our birthdays, his advice, his stand for excellence, his link between God and us, his keeping God at the helm of the family, his insistence on family time and traditions, his private talks and debates with each of us, his pride in his family, and most of all, his love and support for us. I will mostly miss our Sunday morning rendezvous at 8:30, my special time with him every week. There will be an immeasurable void left in our lives.

In his book *Man and Superman*, George Bernard Shaw shared his view on life:

> "This is the true joy in life, the being used for a purpose recognized by yourself as a mighty one; the being thoroughly worn out before you are thrown on the scrap heap; the being a force of Nature instead of a feverish clod of ailments and grievances complaining that the world will not devote itself to making you happy. I am of the opinion that my life belongs to the whole community and as long as I can live, it is my privilege to do for it whatever I can. I want to be thoroughly used up when I die for the harder I work, the more I live. I rejoice in life for its own sake. Life is no brief candle to me. It is sort of a splendid torch which I have got hold of for the moment, and I want to make it burn as brightly as possible before handing it on to future generations."

Papa's life identifies closely with this philosophy of dynamic living. You can tell the quality of a man's life by the legacy he leaves behind. My papa's body is in the coffin, but he lives on. His torch is passed on to his family. You will not see him in the flesh, but you will see and hear him from the pulpit through Zachee, his brother, and Baldwin, my husband. You will listen to his passion for music through Jean and Naasson Jr., his sons. You will feel his compassion, loving care, and healing power for the sick through Rose-Angelle, the nurse, and Marie-Hortense, the physician. You will experience his friendship, love, and generosity through Evangeline's big heart. You will appreciate his charm and beauty through Maud. You will witness his stand of "justice for all" through Jasmine in the courts of law. You will experience his love for his people through Nasson Jr. You will appreciate his creativity through Junith's artistic masterpieces and creative writings. You will see his commitment to excellence and hear his bold speaking for transformation through me, Pollyanna.

His legacy will live on through Maman, for she will keep his torch burning. Papa left a legacy behind that we all can keep alive. You, too, can make a difference with the people you encounter. Love God. Love others. Be passionate about your commitments. This is the only way to live. This is the best way for you to keep his memory alive. This way he lives on through us all.

We are all saddened by this loss. But, let's not "weep as those who have no hope." We have the hope of seeing Papa again in that great day of the coming of the Lord, Jesus Christ. We will be caught up in the sky to meet Jesus and Papa. What a great reunion that will be! I think of the hymn, "When we all get to heaven, what a day of rejoicing that will be. When we all see Jesus, we'll sing and shout VICTORY!" I look forward to that day when we begin our life together again. But this time it will be forever. A BIEN-TOT, PAPA!

ACKNOWLEDGMENTS

This project would not have been realized without the contributions of a village of people who have provided me example, encouragement, love, and support. Although words are not enough to express my sentiments, words are all that I have and the best that I can give. I owe an incredible debt of gratitude to all of you. Merci beaucoup.

I extend my gratitude to the Haitian community who gave back to my father. Merci for your blessings of love and generosity. I also thank my church community for their love and support. Thank you for listening to my stories and giving me feedback on their inspirational effect.

To all my friends, too numerous to list, I thank you for your words of encouragement, love, and prayers. My best female friend, Joy Alexander, visualized the impact of this book. Here it is, Joy. To my dear friend and brilliant designer, Richard White, I cannot repay you in word or reward for your priceless contribution to this book and to many of my other projects. Your excitement, in addition to your work and expert advice, propelled me forward from concept to cover. Merci, merci, merci.

Merci to my in-laws, Drs. Clarence and Sylvia Barnes, for your love and support. My mother-in-law began shaping the rough draft of this manuscript into a book and believed that "such stories should be written in the simplest form such that all who read them may receive a blessing." Being masterful in her craft, I adhered to her suggestions. I hope that the end result is to your satisfaction.

I am blessed to have eight siblings who are my cheerleaders: Rosie, Jean, Evangeline, Naasson Jr., Jasmine, Junith, Maud, and Marie-Hortense. We have a special bond since we all lived the stories from this book together and were all loved by Papa just the same. I thank you so much for your love and untiring support. You are the greatest siblings anyone could ever have. Junith, merci for helping me with the book. Your editing suggestions and ideas were a tremendous contribution. You have the gift of writing, and I look forward to reading your own creations.

I thank my God-fearing parents who practiced what they preached for their children to follow. I am so blessed for having had the privilege of experiencing the stories in this book, and many more, with them. I especially want to thank my mother, Naomie Prosper, a silent giant. Maman, merci for always believing in me. You continue to inspire us to be the best that we can be. I am so proud to be your daughter.

My children, Byron, David, and Gabrielle, are my source of inspiration. I couldn't have asked for better children than you three. You are the best of your father and me, and I am so grateful for who you turned out to be as adults. Your constant acknowledgements have been the fuel that made my creative engine work. Thank you for keeping me going and helping me complete this work. And to Gabrielle, my extraordinary editor and agent, truly, this work has been realized because of your diligent assistance throughout the years. You and I made this book. It is our accomplishment. I have developed a deeper appreciation for your passion for literary works. I cannot thank you enough for the invaluable contributions you made in shaping this book. This is only the beginning. Merci.

To my husband, my best friend, who pushes me to be the best that I can be, I owe an immeasurable debt of gratitude. He is my anchor. In him I find a well of inspiration that causes me to rise beyond my own expectations and re-invent myself. Every moment lived with you is a once-in-a-lifetime adventure. Thank you for your love and support.

MERCI BEAUCOUP!

ABOUT THE AUTHOR

Pollyanna Prosper-Barnes, Ph.D., was born in Port-au-Prince, Haiti, to Christian parents, Naasson and Naomie Prosper. During her career, she has taught and administered in various educational systems from kindergarten to graduate levels. This experience has provided her an opportunity to make a difference in the lives of those she serves. Pollyanna has served the Northeastern Conference of Seventh-day Adventists as superintendent of schools and director of children's ministries. She states that, "Through education we create a world of possibilities for our young people and give them tools to turn possibility into reality."

Pollyanna is married to her college sweetheart, Baldwin Barnes, pastor of the City Tabernacle church in Manhattan. They are blessed with three young-adult children.

Pollyanna is a dynamic, transformational speaker and inspirational writer. Her passionate presentations inspire thousands throughout the U.S. and abroad to live up to their full potential in every facet of life. One of her passions is to motivate people to tap into the gifts that God gave them. She is a stand for their greatness and is committed to empowering them to develop a deeper relationship with God.

Pollyanna is a woman of God who has completely surrendered her life to His service.

Breinigsville, PA USA
03 June 2010
239161BV00003B/2/P

9 781572 586208